POISON PLANTS

BY ALAN ESHLEMAN

With original illustrations by Kristin Jakob

Houghton Mifflin Company Boston 1977

For Carol and Jason

Acknowledgments

To all the people who helped me write this book, I offer my heartfelt thanks. Thanks to my father, John Eshleman, who first showed me how to write. Thanks also to Al Molina, my first botany teacher; to Dr. Robert Ornduff, director of the Jepson Herbarium, University of California, Berkeley; to Dr. Guy Hartman; to the staff of the Lowie Museum of Anthropology; to the staff of the Royal Botanical Gardens at Kew, England; and to Harold Silverman, who encouraged me to write about poisonous plants. Finally, my thanks to Dr. John Kingsbury of Cornell University. I have never met Professor Kingsbury, but his book *Poisonous Plants of the United States and Canada* and his other scientific writings have taught me a great deal about the subject.

Library of Congress Cataloging in Publication Data

Eshleman, Alan.
 Poison plants.

 SUMMARY: Discusses about thirty poisonous plants, their toxic effects on humans and animals, and how they can be used beneficially.
 1. Poisonous plants — Juvenile literature.   2. Poisonous plants — Toxicology — Juvenile literature.
 [1. Poisonous plants]   I. Jakob, Kristin.   II. Title.
 QK100.A1E83   581.6'9   77-14176
 ISBN 0-395-25298-9

V 10 9 8 7 6 5 4 3 2 1

CONTENTS

To the Reader

There are more than 30,000 different kinds of plants growing in the United States, of which about 700 are known to be poisonous to human beings or to animals. If I were to describe all of these poisonous plants, this would be a very thick book indeed. In addition to some 700 detailed descriptions, it would also have to include a complete course in botany — the science of plants — to help you understand all the technical words in the descriptions. My major reason for writing this book was *not* to teach you how to identify plants. Instead, I wanted to share the story of poisonous plants with you — to relate something of the history of these plants and to show their importance in the modern world. However, if you do want to learn how to identify poisonous plants you will not be disappointed, because I have included pictures and descriptions of many poisonous plants found in the United States and in other parts of the world. I hope that these descriptions will be good enough to aid you in identifying some of the more common and widespread poisonous plants, especially the ones that you are likely to see in the wild or to find in your home or garden.

One of my most difficult tasks in writing this book was deciding which plants to include and which to leave out. There are simply too many fascinating, dangerous, and useful poisonous plants in the world to include all of them in a book of this size. I have tried instead to choose plants that illustrate the many different kinds of plant poisons. Some of these plants are dangerous to human beings, some are dangerous to animals, and many are dangerous to both. Some of the plants are quite deadly, while others — poison ivy, for example — are more of a nuisance than a threat. Quite a few of these poisonous plants are also the source of valuable medicines.

For each of the plants discussed I have given both the common and the scientific (Latin) names. I hope that you will not be scared by the scientific names. If you are inspired to go on to learn more about poisonous plants (as I hope you will be), you will find the scientific names very useful. Many of the more technical books about poisonous plants do not even include common names. Here are a few general rules for using scientific names:

Every scientific name has two parts; scientific names are sometimes called *binomials*, which means "two names." The first part of the scientific name is the *genus*, or generic, name. The genus name always begins with a capital letter. The second part of the name is the *species*, or specific, name. The species name always begins with a lower-case letter. For example, the scientific name of poison ivy is *Rhus radicans* (genus *Rhus*, species *radicans*). Many different plants may have the same genus name if they are closely related to each other. For example, poison oak and poison sumac are also members of the genus *Rhus*. Poison oak is *Rhus diversiloba* and poison sumac is *Rhus vernix*. Groups of closely related genera (*genera* is the plural of *genus*) make up a family. Poison oak, poison ivy, and poison sumac are all members of the Sumac family. Sometimes scientific names are abbreviated by writing the initial of the genus name followed by the full species name, for example, *R. radicans* for poison ivy.

The major advantage to using scientific names is that they help avoid confusion. Consider the poisonous plant called St. John's Wort. In some parts of the United States this same plant is known as Klamath weed. But to botanists, the plant is always

Hypericum perforatum. A botanist in Japan or France or the Soviet Union or in any other part of the world may not know what "St. John's Wort" means, but he or she will know the plant by its scientific name. Scientific names are a kind of international language.

Scientific names also help to clear up the confusion that results when several different plants have the same common name. For example, in the United States at least three different plants are known as "skunk cabbage." The scientific names, *Lysichiton americanum, Symplocarpus foetidus,* and *Veratrum californicum* clearly show that they are different plants.

Finally, it should be noted that poisonous plants are a far greater threat to animals, especially grazing animals, than they are to human beings. Few of you, however, will encounter these particular plants, so this book emphasizes the plants that are dangerous to people.

PART ONE

1

Introduction

A man is moving silently through the tropical forest, slipping in and out of the shadows of the dense growth. He is hunting. The forest too is silent — the only sounds that can be heard are the high-pitched buzz of an insect and the distant cry of a wild parrot. Suddenly the man freezes. There, seventy-five feet above him, sitting on the limb of a tree, is a monkey. The monkey has not seen the man.

Quickly, the man reaches into a leather pouch strapped around his waist and takes out a small wooden dart. Never taking his eyes off the monkey, he slips the dart into a slender wooden tube. He raises the tube to his lips as if it were a giant peashooter. Then, in a split second, his cheeks bulge out and, with a hiss of air, the dart flies from the tube, sails up through the jungle trees, and sticks in the monkey's hip.

For a second, the animal does not move. Then its brown eyes go wide with terror and it jumps from branch to branch, sailing twenty feet through the air. Suddenly the monkey loses its grip and falls toward the jungle floor, bouncing off branches, and finally landing with a soft thud. The jungle forest is full of noise as branches rattle, birds scream, and other monkeys chatter. The hunter walks over to the fallen monkey. The animal is still alive and gasping for breath, but as the hunter watches, the monkey's chest heaves a few times and then stops. It is dead.

How can this be? The dart cut the animal, but it did not make a serious wound — certainly not serious enough to kill. But it was not the dart that killed the monkey. It was something *on* the dart. The dart was poisoned.

A few hours before he went hunting, in his village deep in the jungle of Guiana in South America, the hunter had dipped his darts into a bowl of special poison prepared by his tribe's own medicine man. The medicine man had promised the hunter good luck if he used poison darts, and he had been right.

I am lucky, thinks the hunter, for this monkey will feed my wife, my children, and my mother-in-law, and there will still be some left for the medicine man. He lifts the animal across his shoulders and walks back to his village.

Three thousand miles north of the Guiana jungle, a helicopter flies across the North Texas plains. Scattered across the plain below are hundreds of head of cattle. The helicopter dives low over the herd, frightening the cattle and causing them to stampede.

The helicopter continues to circle over the same spot as the pilot looks for something. Then he sees what he has been hoping not to find: below him are seven cows that have not run. Instead, they lie motionless in the grass. They are dead.

The pilot shakes his head sadly as he lands his craft, then begins walking across the prairie, stopping every few feet to pull up clumps of grass and weeds and put them in a plastic bag. Then he walks back to the helicopter. Inside the cockpit, he switches on a radio transmitter and speaks into a microphone:

"Double R Ranch. Double R Ranch. This is Tony. Come in."

"Double R here, Tony," answers the loudspeaker. "This is Jimmy. We read you loud and clear. What's up?"

"Jimmy, we have seven dead steers near Willow Creek. Looks like locoweed. I've got some plants for the vet to look at."

"Roger, Tony. That makes nineteen we've lost this month. Put up a flag and I'll send out a truck."

"Roger. Over and out."

Tony switches off the radio, reaches behind his seat, and pulls out some aluminum poles and a bright orange flag. He walks over to the dead cattle, fits the aluminum poles together to make a single long flagpole, ties the flag to one end, and then jabs the pole into the soft dirt. The orange flag flaps in the prairie breeze for the truck driver to see when he comes to haul away the steers.

Now Tony steps back into the cockpit and starts the engine. The rotor blades turn faster and faster until the helicopter rises from the prairie in a thick cloud of dust. The aircraft banks sharply and whirls away to the southwest. In a few minutes the helicopter is gone over the horizon and the prairie is quiet.

Two thousand miles to the east, in a New Jersey hospital, a doctor waits impatiently outside a laboratory. Two hours earlier, a young woman was brought to the hospital suffering from terrible stomach pains. The night before she had eaten a stew containing wild mushrooms she had gathered herself. Some of the mushrooms had been poisonous, but what kind were they?

The doctor must know so he can select the proper treatment, for if he uses the wrong drugs it can be very serious. Now the laboratory door opens and a man steps out.

"It's an *Amanita*," says the man emerging from the laboratory, "the worst kind."

The doctor looks worried. He walks down the corridor and into a hospital room where the young woman is lying in bed. Her face is pale. She is in great pain.

"Can you hear me," asks the doctor.

"Yes," she whispers. "Can you make it stop hurting?"

"I'll try," says the doctor. "You ate a poisonous mushroom. I want to give you a new drug that will make you better, but I'll need your permission to use it. It's still experimental. Do you understand?"

"Yes, I understand. What happens if you don't use the drug?"

"To be very honest," says the doctor, "you could die."

"Then yes, please use it."

Two weeks later, in the same hospital room, the young woman is sitting up in bed. She is smiling and her cheeks are full of color. The doctor is standing by the bed.

"You saved my life," she says. "Was it a close call?"

"Yes," replies the doctor, "you were very lucky. Next time, I hope you'll gather mushrooms at the supermarket."

Three very different situations — the hunter, the pilot, and the mushroom gatherer — but each involving poisonous plants. The hunter in the South American jungle was using darts that had been dipped in *curare*, a powerful poison obtained from the roots of certain jungle vines. The dead cattle on the Texas plain had been grazing on locoweed, an herb that is a member of the pea family. And the young woman in New Jersey had eaten the most poisonous mushrooom known, *Amanita phalloides*, the terrible "destroying angel." How common are incidents like these, and how big a problem are poisonous plants?

This is a difficult question to answer for two reasons. First, many cases of plant poisoning never come to the attention of doctors, especially if the symptoms are not severe. Second, doctors are not legally required to report cases of plant poisoning to their local health departments (as they must do for infectious diseases such as tuberculosis or typhoid fever). Since most cases of plant poisoning are not fatal, most are never reported.

By far the best and most recent statistics of human poisoning by plants are those gathered during 1974 by the National Clearinghouse for Poison Control Centers. These centers are part of the United States Food and Drug Administration. In 1974, 161,557 cases of possible poison ingestion (swallowing) were reported to the centers. Of these 161,557 cases, the top three categories of poison were:

> Medicines (78,061 cases)
> Cleaning and polishing agents (20,571 cases)
> Plants (11,097 cases)

These figures must be looked at cautiously, though, because not every "case" was actually poisoned. To be counted as a case, all that was necessary was for a person to swallow a plant that was *suspected* of being poisonous. For example, 422 of these cases involved *Pyracantha* berries. These berries taste awful, but they are not dangerous. Of course, many of these cases did involve truly poisonous plants. Most cases of plant poisoning are never reported to the Poison Control Centers so it is difficult to estimate the total. However, it is likely that the majority of cases are never reported. Some medical authorities have estimated that the true number of cases of plant poisoning in the United States is between 50,000 and 100,000 per year.

Eight out of every ten cases of plant ingestion reported to the Poison Control Centers were children less than five years of age, infants and toddlers who are not old enough to understand the danger of putting unfamiliar objects into their mouths. Among these young children, plants were the *number one* suspected poison (7351 cases), followed by soaps and detergents (5474 cases) and aspirin (4837 cases).

Nineteen seventy-four was the first year since the Food and Drug Administration began collecting poison reports that plants headed the list of poisonous substances swallowed by children. In all previous years aspirin had been number one. There are two reasons for this switch. First, the number of cases of accidental aspirin poisoning have been steadily declining since the introduction of "childproof" caps on aspirin bottles. Second, the number of cases of accidental poisoning among young children appears to be increasing.

Of course, there is no way to be absolutely sure that plant poisoning among children is increasing. It may only be that doctors are becoming more aware of poisonous plants and are therefore reporting the cases more often, but there are strong clues that the increase is real. The table opposite lists the top ten poisonous plants reported to Poison Control Centers during 1965 and 1974. (The 1974 list is the most recent available.)

Some of the plants on this list are not truly poisonous, honeysuckle and pyracantha, for example. Other plants are not named with precision: pokeweed, philodendron, and nightshade are names that have been given to both poisonous and nonpoisonous species (this is why scientific names are so important). But one big difference between the two years is that there are more *house plants* on the 1974 list, such as dieffenbachia,

	1965	1974
1.	Pokeweed	Philodendron
2.	Yew	Yew
3.	Philodendron	Pyracantha
4.	Bittersweet	Woody nightshade (=Bittersweet?)
5.	Nightshade (species not given)	Marijuana
6.	Holly (berries)	Holly (berries)
7.	Honeysuckle	Poinsettia
8.	Pyracantha	Dieffenbachia
9.	Castor bean	Black elderberry
10.	Jerusalem cherry	Oleander

poinsettia, and philodendron. House plants have become very popular in the last few years, and it is probably this phenomenon, more than any other, that is responsible for the increase of accidental plant poisoning among young children.

Poisonous plants are also a major problem for farmers and ranchers. Each year, throughout the world, hundreds of thousands of cattle, sheep, goats, pigs, and other domestic animals die from eating poisonous plants. A veterinarian who treats farm animals will see more cases of plant poisoning in a single year than most doctors who treat human patients will see in their entire lifetime.

A very small proportion of the plant kingdom is poisonous. Less than 1 per cent of the 500,000 known species of plants growing on the earth are harmful to human beings or animals. But why are there any poisonous plants at all? People have been asking this question for thousands of years.

Some people believe that poisonous plants use their poisons for protection, to help in their struggle for survival, much as a rattlesnake uses its venom to destroy enemies. But before most plant poisons can take effect, the plants themselves must be eaten. Of what protective value is a poison to a plant if the plant must be destroyed in order to protect itself? So protection is probably *not* the answer.

Plants may be thought of as complicated chemical factories. Using minerals from the soil, carbon dioxide from the air, and light from the sun, green plants are able to manufacture their own food and all the other materials that they need to live. A typical plant manufactures hundreds of different chemical compounds according to a very complicated and specific plan known as the "genetic code." The genetic code is stored in every plant cell in the form of a complex molecule called *deoxyribose nucleic acid* (DNA, for short). Because this code is so complicated, mistakes sometimes occur. The mistakes are called "mutations." Some mutations cause plants to assemble chemical compounds that are seemingly of no value to the plant. If these compounds are harmful to the plant, the plant will die before it has a chance to produce seeds and make new plants. But if the compound is not harmful to the plant, there is a good chance that the plant will live long enough to produce seeds and thereby pass along its "mistake" to future generations. Some of these compounds produced by mutation may be highly poisonous to animals while having no effect at all on the plant. For example, a deadly poison called strychnine comes from a tropical vine called *Strychnos nux-vomica*. Strychnine has absolutely no effect on the plant, but if eaten by a person or an animal it will cause paralysis or death. Nicotine, a chemical found in tobacco (and in cigarettes), is poisonous to insects and, in sufficient amounts, to human beings. Yet nicotine has no effect on the tobacco plant. In fact, scientists have grown healthy tobacco plants that contain no nicotine at all. The process of growing nicotine-free tobacco is very expensive, for it involves grafting the stem of a tobacco plant to the roots of another species. This is why tobacco farmers do not produce nicotine-free tobacco.

Of course, it is impossible to say for certain that a poisonous chemical is truly useless to a plant. In time we may discover that many plant poisons serve important functions in the plants that manufacture them, but for the time being the most honest answer to the question "Why are there poisonous plants?" is simply that nobody knows.

2

A Short History
of Poisonous Plants

I*t is very likely* that human beings have known about poisonous
plants throughout the history of man — by the latest estimates,
for at least a million years.

The first people on earth fed themselves with what they could
gather from the land and from the waters. They did not raise
crops or tend herds of cattle. Agriculture is a fairly recent development, having been started by the human race perhaps no
more than ten thousand years ago. Our earliest ancestors ate
the fruits and foliage of wild plants and hunted and fished for
their meat. Theirs was not always an easy life: they seldom
lived longer than thirty years; death in infancy was common;
and a person was considered middle-aged as a teen-ager.

When food was scarce, perhaps during times of drought or
other extreme weather conditions, prehistoric people must have
been forced to experiment with new and unfamiliar foods. If
the food was a poisonous plant, the result of the experiment
could have been illness or even death.

Imagine a small tribe of primitive people making their way
across a dry plain, searching for food. It has been more than
two days since any of them have eaten and they are very hungry:

the young children are crying, while the older members of the tribe grit their teeth and try to ignore the pain in their own stomachs. What is there to eat? Nothing. Nothing but dry grass and the branches of trees. Suddenly one of the tribesmen makes a discovery: there, not far away, is a bush covered with fat, ripe berries. It is a strange plant — nobody in the tribe has seen one like it before. The leaders of the tribe try to convince the others not to eat from the strange bush, for they are well aware of what might happen. But some cannot resist. They are hungry and the berries look good, so they eat.

A few hours later all of those who ate the strange berries are sick. They complain of pain and burn with fever. Night comes, but the sufferers cannot sleep. They thrash and cry out, begging the evil spirits in the plant to let them alone. By the next morning a few have died, while some of the others are feeling a little better. By the next day the dead have been buried and the survivors are well enough to move on with the rest of the tribe, still searching for food. All of the survivors remember the poisonous bush in great detail. They remember its leaves, the shape and color of its berries, the pattern of its branches, and a dozen other details. The strange plant has been added to the tribe's common knowledge and will not be forgotten.

Prehistoric people must also have learned about poisonous plants from watching animals. When they saw that an animal avoided a certain plant or became sick after eating it, the early hunters must have begun to suspect that the plant had poisonous properties. Seeing that animals sometimes died after eating particular plants must have given these people the idea of using these plants on their hunts; dipping spears and arrows in the juices of the plants allowed them to kill wild animals more easily.

The same idea must have come to people all over the primitive world, because the use of plant poisons for hunting and fishing is widespread. In many parts of Africa, spear and arrow poisons are made from the fruits and bark of the so-called poison tree, *Ackonthera venenata*. In Central and South America, the native Indians prepare a powerful arrow poison called curare (cue-*rah*-ree) from the roots of *Chondodendron* and *Strophanthus* vines. In Europe and Asia wolfbane, or monkshood (*Aconitum napellum*), was used as an arrow poison. The word *toxin*, which means "poison," comes from the old Greek word *toxon*, meaning "bow," indicating the long association of poison with hunting weapons.

According to a legend of the Nandi tribe of eastern Africa, the poison tree was discovered by a poor woman who was walking through the forest gathering food for her two children. Under a tree she found a dead bird, which she took home and fed to her two children. The children became very sick after eating the bird, but they did not die. When they had recovered, the woman went again to the tree where she had found the bird and rubbed the tip of an arrow in the juice from its fruits. Then she gave the arrow to her son and asked him to shoot an animal. The boy did as his mother asked, but his shot was off its mark and the animal received only a flesh wound. Yet, surprisingly enough, the animal died. Soon all the hunters in the tribe were using arrows dipped in the juice of the poison tree. As a result, the tribe became very rich. Though this is only a legend, it is probably very close to the truth.

Our knowledge of how prehistoric people used poisonous plants is based on a few clues and many educated guesses. Some of it is based on the work of anthropologists who have studied the primitive cultures that still exist in some parts of the world. These cultures, the anthropologists suspect, use plants in much the same way their ancestors did. Archaeologists have uncovered seeds, traces of pollen, and other fragments of plants among the remains of ancient settlements. By using delicate chemical tests, scientists have been able to tell how long ago these plants were harvested. Some of the remains are very old indeed. It is probably safe to say that most of the major poisonous plants were discovered by primitive people tens of thousands of years ago.

Our remote ancestors must have developed quite a sophisticated knowledge of the plants that were growing around them. Today, when scientists go into remote areas of the world to observe and study primitive cultures, they are often amazed by how well these people know their plants. Not only do they know that some plants are poisonous, but they also know that certain parts of these plants are more poisonous than others. They know that some plants are dangerous only at certain times of the year and that in other plants the poisons can be removed, making them safe to eat. In tropical South America the cassava is an important source of food, despite the fact that it contains dangerous amounts of hydrocyanic acid. Long ago the native Indians learned how to cook the poison out of the cassava before eating it. (We, in North America, sometimes eat the cassava in the form of tapioca pudding.)

Many of the plant poisons that are applied to spears and arrows require lengthy preparation: they must be boiled and concentrated until they are powerful enough to stop an animal in its tracks and then mixed with other plant substances that will make the poisons stick to the weapon. All of this suggests that primitive people must have conducted many experiments with poisonous plants.

Early people also discovered that some plants could cure illnesses. Many of these medicinal plants were poisonous, but early medicine men somehow understood the delicate balance between the amounts they could give their patients to help them and the amounts that would be harmful. Several of the drugs used in modern medicine were first discovered by "primitive" people. Indians in South America have long known that the bark of the "fever tree," *Cinchona*, would cure malaria. After hundreds of years of skepticism, western medicine adopted *Cinchona* bark as an antimalarial drug more widely known as quinine. Chulmoogra oil, from the bark of the kalaw tree of Southeast Asia, has been used successfully to cure leprosy, a cure that had been mentioned in native legends for hundreds of years before the drug was finally "discovered" by western doctors.

There have been so many instances of native herbal cures having real medicinal value that some scientists have devoted their energies toward seeking out promising new medicinal plants. As part of the effort to find a cure for cancer, the United States Department of Agriculture sends explorers throughout the world to search out and collect plants that may have antitumor properties.

Sometime between six and eight thousand years ago, the first written language was developed in the land between the Tigris and Euphrates rivers, the site of modern Iraq. In time, many other civilizations developed written languages — Chinese, Sanskrit, Mayan, and Egyptian. The written records that remain show ample evidence that all of these civilizations were well acquainted with poisonous plants.

Five thousand years ago Egyptian physicians assembled a vast collection of drugs that were extracted from plants. Many of these plants were also poisonous. A fragment of Egyptian papyrus, perhaps three thousand years old, bears the inscription: "Pronounce not the name IAO under the penalty of the peach." We can only guess as to who or what "IAO" was, but we can be reasonably sure that "the peach" referred to hydrocyanic acid, a deadly poison that can be extracted from the leaves and the stones of the peach.

During the five centuries before the birth of Christ, Greek medicine was the most advanced in the world, and the most famous Greek physician was Hippocrates of Cos. Hippocrates is best known as the author of the Hippocratic oath, a code of conduct for doctors that is still recited in medical schools to this very day. One of the lines of the Hippocratic oath reads: "I will give no deadly drug to any, though it be asked of me, nor will I counsel such . . ." Yet the doctors of Hippocrates' time routinely gave their patients doses of very poisonous plants. Hippocrates himself sometimes prescribed extracts of the opium poppy and of the black hellebore to relieve his patients' pain, and he used an extract of the mandrake as an anesthetic for eye surgery. Obviously Hippocrates and his fellow physicians had some idea of what the proper dose should be.

One of the most influential books about plants that has survived from ancient Greece is the *Historia Plantarum* (*History of Plants*) by the scholar Theophrastus. Theophrastus was a student of the philosopher Aristotle, who was also a botanist of no small accomplishment. Upon Aristotle's death, his student inherited Aristotle's collection of botanical books and papers and became custodian of his garden. As custodian, Theophrastus conducted a variety of research with plants, research that has earned him the title "father of botany." Among his many discoveries was the first notice of sexual reproduction in flowering plants. Theophrastus' garden included many poisonous plants.

During the first century A.D. Dioscorides, personal physician to the infamous Roman emperor Nero, published *De Materia Medica* (*On Medicinal Matters*), which listed some six hundred plant species of medicinal value, including many poisonous species. *De Materia Medica* was another enormously influential book. Widely translated and reprinted, it was consulted by physicians until well after the American Revolution, some seventeen hundred years later.

Medicine was not the only use for poisonous plants during Theophrastus' and Dioscorides' days. Poisons, and especially poisons from poisonous plants, were the favorite weapon of murderers. During Roman times there were actually professional poisoners — the equivalent of today's underworld "hit men" — who would kill anyone for the right price. Most frequently the poisons would be placed in the victim's food or drink. The professional poisoners developed special recipes, using honey or fragrant spices to disguise the bitter taste and unpleasant odors characteristic of many plants. These recipes were jealously guarded trade secrets.

Usually the motive for poisoning was political. Roman noblemen, senators, generals, and even the emperor himself were targets. The fear of poisoning was so great among the ruling classes of ancient Greece and Rome that special jobs were created for people to see to it that no poison found its way into foods. The position of chef in a nobleman's household was one of great power and trust. Sometimes the household would employ tasters, whose sole responsibility was to sample all foods before they were served and attempt to detect the presence of poisons. At banquets the taster would sample the food in full view of the guests to reassure them that it was safe to eat. If the food was suspect, it might be served to dogs, and then the animals would be carefully watched to see if they developed symptoms of poisoning. Another trusted member of the noble household was the cupbearer, whose job was to see that his employer's wine was not poisoned between the cask and the table.

For more than a thousand years after the decline of Rome, poisons remained the favorite weapon of political assassination.

The ways in which poisons were given to victims became more and more ingenious. Douw Steyn has described some of these methods in *The Toxiciology of Plants in South Africa*. Poisons, he writes, were applied to knives, forks, or toothpicks that were to be used by the victim; fumes from burning plants might be pumped into rooms occupied by the victim; and sometimes poisons were mixed with oils and fats and rubbed into the victim's skin while he slept. In Shakespeare's great tragedy *Hamlet*, King Hamlet of Denmark is killed by a potion from a poisonous plant that is poured into his ear while he sleeps. In the same play, his son, Prince Hamlet, is killed by a poison-tipped sword. "In the sixteenth and seventeenth century," writes Dr. Steyn, "rings fitted with poisoned needles were worn, and a scratch from these poisoned rings resulted in the deaths of the wearer's enemies."

During the Renaissance — from the fourteenth to the seventeenth centuries — societies of professional poisoners flourished in Italy. Like their counterparts during Roman times, these poisoners found their major employment in removing various political enemies. The records of the city council of Venice for 1514 report that a Franciscan monk, John of Ragubo, was hired to poison the Holy Roman Emperor Maximilian. If successful, Brother John was to receive an annual pension of some fifteen hundred gold ducats. History has recorded that Brother John was not successful, but the minutes of the Venice council do indicate that other poisoners were successfully hired to eliminate less powerful political enemies.

The most vicious use of plant poisons occurred in times of war, when opposing armies tried to poison each other's water supplies. The most recent example of this kind of warfare comes from the late nineteenth century, when the Indian army poisoned wells with monkshood in an attempt to stop the advancing British army.

The early Greek and Roman physicians had extensive collections of drugs that they prescribed as antidotes to poison. Two of the most popular antidotes were bezoar stones and mithridaticum, or theriaca. Bezoar stones were one of two things: either balls of hair and mucus taken from the stomachs of oxen or the gallstones of cattle. Mithridaticum was a complicated mixture of more than sixty ingredients first developed by King Mithridates of Pontus around 100 B.C. Both bezoar stones and mithridaticum are now known to be worthless antidotes, yet both enjoyed great popularity for hundreds of years.

King Mithridates had been trained in Greek medicine and devoted a substantial portion of his energies to a search for an antidote that might protect against all poisons, the so-called universal antidote. He sometimes used slaves in his experiments, first feeding these unfortunate people some poison, then giving them some of his antidote and recording the results. When Mithridates' kingdom was conquered by the Romans in 53 B.C., the recipe for the universal antidote was discovered in the king's medical library. This recipe was quickly passed to Roman physicians, who altered it slightly, gave it the name theriaca, and spread the word of this remarkable "antidote" throughout the empire. In *Poisoning Misadventures* Dr. Lloyd Jensen writes of theriac:

> It was hailed as a cure-all for all diseases and conditions, as well as an antidote for all poisons. Theriaca became the most famous medicine or cure-all ever known, and was used widely from 70 A.D. to 1870 A.D. The people of the Middle Ages dosed themselves with theriaca to cure toothache, plague, "leprosy," battle wounds, and so on. They had blind faith in "theriac," that wonderful placebo.

What was this marvelous cure-all? Again quoting Dr. Jensen:

24

Over the centuries, the formulae varied greatly, but of the sixty-two ingredients listed in Europe, the mainstays were gentian root, hyssop, clarified butter, nutmeg, Illyrian iris, incense, myrrh, spikenard, balm of Gilead, Dead Sea bitumen, red earth from Lemnos . . . honey, opium, and dried viper flesh.

Perhaps theriaca owed much of its popularity to one ingredient, opium, which surely dulled any pain the user might have been feeling. Certainly the presence of opium explains the drug's popularity as a toothache remedy. As recently as 1960 theriaca was still being sold in a drugstore in Venice.

The modern era in the study of poisonous plants, and of poisons in general, began in the eighteenth century with the development of chemistry. Scientists at this time were learning more than ever before about the composition of all manner of things, animal, vegetable, and mineral. By the early nineteenth century, chemists were able to isolate the poisonous chemicals found in wolfbane, henbane, belladonna, and many other poisonous plants.

In 1814 the Spanish chemist Matthew Orfila published his *Treatise on Toxicology,* in which he summarized most of what was then known about poisons. Orfila's greatest contribution was to show that poisons tend to concentrate in different parts of the body — in the brain, the liver, or the kidneys, for example. Before Orfila's pioneering experiments, it was common practice for doctors to look only at the contents of a suspected poisoning victim's stomach. If no poison was found, poisoning would often be ruled out as the cause of death. Orfila showed that traces of poison could be found in other organs. This new knowledge helped to reduce the use of poisons as murder weapons because it made the crime harder to conceal.

3

How Do Poisons Work?

To *understand how poisons work* requires that one first understand the process called *metabolism*. All life may be thought of as the result of a complex series of chemical reactions. The energy we use when we move our bodies was extracted from the food we eat by a chemical process called *respiration*. When we gain or lose weight we do so because of chemical reactions. The impulses that move through our nerves are actually high-speed chemical reactions. All of these chemical reactions, and the hundreds of others that keep us alive, when taken together are called metabolism. As long as the chemical reactions of metabolism take place normally, living things are healthy, but if anything interferes with the reactions, illness may result. A poison, according to this scheme, is simply a special chemical that interferes with metabolism.

Most plant poisons fall into one or more of five major categories, according to the ways in which they interfere with metabolism. Briefly, they are: nerve poisons, internal organ poisons, irritants, allergy producers, and mineral poisons.

NERVE POISONS

Some of the most poisonous plants known produce nerve poisons. The water hemlock, belladonna, foxglove, and the curares all fall into this group. Nerve poisons are actually a very diverse group of toxins, because the nervous system itself is a very complex thing. Some nerves, known as the *somatic nervous system,* go to the striated muscles — the muscles that are under conscious control, such as the muscles of the arms and legs. Other nerves, the *autonomic nervous system,* control the smooth muscles and the muscles of the heart — muscles that are not usually under conscious control. The autonomic nervous system controls the muscles of the stomach, the intestines, the uterus, and several other organs. Still other nerves make up the *central nervous system,* the nerves of the brain and the spinal cord.

Scientists classify nerve poisons according to which part of the nervous system they interfere with. For example, the poisons from the curares and the red tides affect the somatic nervous system. Ergot, belladonna, jimsonweed, and several other plants interfere with the autonomic nervous system. Opium is a poisonous plant that acts on the central nervous system.

The greatest danger with nerve poisoning is that the nerves that control breathing will fail. If this happens, the victim will die of asphyxiation. The doctor's most important task in treating a victim of nerve poisoning is making sure that the patient continues to breathe until all of the poison has been removed from his body.

INTERNAL ORGAN POISONS

Internal organ poisons affect such organs as the stomach, liver, and kidneys. The effects of some of these poisons are very mild, producing no more than an upset stomach, while others can be quite deadly. One of the worst internal plant poisons is produced by the deadly amanita mushroom. Amanita poisons destroy the living tissue of the liver, so that even after the poison has left the body the victim is still in mortal danger of death from liver failure. Several plants, including peach trees, cassava, and hydrangea, produce the powerful chemical cyanide. The major effect of cyanide is to prevent oxygen from entering living cells. Victims of cyanide poisoning may be able to breathe and yet still die of asphyxiation.

IRRITANTS

Several poisonous plants produce caustic chemicals that can burn the skin and eyes. If these chemicals are swallowed they may do great damage to the mouth and throat. The manchineel tree, which grows in southern Florida and on many Caribbean islands, is one plant that produces a strong irritant.

ALLERGY PRODUCERS (ALLERGENS)

Poisonous plants can be divided into two major groups, the *truly poisonous plants* and the *allergy-producing plants*. All of the plants that I have mentioned so far in this chapter belong to the first group. The truly poisonous plants contain poisons that are harmful to *everyone* that comes in contact with them. In contrast, the allergy-producing plants do not cause unpleasant symptoms for everybody. A bad reaction to an allergy-producing plant requires only that a person have an unusually high sensitivity to it.

Most of you have allergies of one kind or another. Perhaps your doctor has advised you not to eat shellfish or chocolate because they cause allergic reactions that make it hard for you to breathe. Certainly you know someone who has an allergy — someone who can't drink cow's milk without breaking out in a rash or who can't be in the same room with a cat without going into violent sneezing fits. One thing you've probably noticed about allergies is that not everybody has the same one. In fact, it's true to say that people's allergy patterns are about as distinctive as their fingerprints — no two are the same. Yet one allergy is shared by more than half the people in the United States: more than 100 million people are allergic to a plant called poison ivy. (Of course, this doesn't mean that 100 million people *get* poison ivy; most people never come in contact with it during their entire lives.)

The rash and itching caused by the poison ivy plant are actually allergic reactions. When the sticky sap of the plant is absorbed by the skin, the body begins to manufacture substances called *antibodies*, which attach themselves to the chemicals in the poison ivy sap and prevent them from moving freely about our bodies. If you are allergic to poison ivy, your body tends to overreact to the presence of the sap. In such instances, enormous amounts of antibodies are produced. These antibodies, in turn, produce large amounts of *histamines*, which cause the body tissue to become inflamed and swollen.

Hay fever is another plant allergy that usually develops when a person has an unusually high sensitivity to the pollen of flowering plants. Less well known is the fact that about 15 per cent of all hay fever cases are actually allergies to the spores of fungi.

MINERAL POISONS

Some plants, which are themselves not poisonous, may become poisonous after absorbing large quantities of toxic minerals from the soil or from the air. These plants are called *accumulators*. Some of the most important plants in this group have the ability to absorb the chemical element selenium. For reasons that are not well understood, many of these plants require large amounts of selenium for normal growth. When farm animals eat these plants they are poisoned. One form of selenium poisoning, known as the "blind staggers," occurs in cattle. The poor animals wander aimlessly about their pastures until they finally die from failure to breathe. Another form of selenium poisoning — "alkali poisoning" — causes horses, cattle, and sheep to develop deformed hoofs and severe anemia. In the United States, selenium poisoning of livestock is often caused by grazing on plants from the genus *Astragalus*, small, shrubby members of the pea family. The selenium-accumulating species of *Astragalus* are sometimes referred to as "locoweeds," although true locoweeds are not selenium accumulators but rather poisonous plants in their own right.

Selenium sometimes occurs in soils along with another element, uranium. Prospectors have taken advantage of this relationship by searching for selenium-accumulating plants and then testing the soil for the presence of uranium. There have been a few lucky prospectors who "struck it rich" after digging beneath a clump of *Astragalus*.

Many of the plants that grow beside busy roads and highways contain large amounts of the poisonous element lead, which comes from automobile exhaust. Most gasoline contains a compound called *tetraethyl lead*, which is used to boost the performance of the engine and eliminate "knock." When leaded gasoline is burned in automobile engines, most of the lead is sprayed out of the exhaust pipe. Some of this lead settles directly onto the leaves and stems of roadside plants. Other lead falls to the soil and is later taken into plants through their roots. Some roadside plants contain so much lead that they are potentially dangerous to grazing animals.

We've all watched the scene in a movie or a television show:

an unsuspecting victim drinks from a poisoned cup. Within seconds he realizes that something is terribly wrong. First he stares at the cup; then as he realizes what has happened his eyes begin to show fear. He gasps for breath but his lungs are tight; he tries to stand, but his legs are rubbery. Within seconds he crashes to the floor, dragging a lamp or tablecloth or potted plant with him. He is dead.

While it is true that some poisons take effect quickly, very few natural plant poisons kill as swiftly as whatever was in the actor's cup. Most plant poisons in their natural form — that is, poisons that have not been extracted from the plant — take hours to act. Some even take days or weeks before their toxic effects are felt. On the other hand, poisons that have been extracted from plants can be much faster-acting because they are more concentrated. Many of the poisonous mushrooms begin to cause unpleasant symptoms three or four hours after they have been eaten. However, the most deadly mushroom, *Amanita phalloides*, rarely causes any symptoms for at least twelve hours after being eaten. Doctors use these time differences to help make diagnoses. If a person begins experiencing unpleasant symptoms within a few hours after eating mushrooms, it is fairly certain that he will survive. If the symptoms come twelve or more hours after the meal, it is a cause for much concern.

The amount of plant material necessary to cause symptoms of poisoning is highly variable. Some of this variation is due to the plants themselves. Different plants within the same species may contain different amounts of poison. The amount of sunlight reaching a plant, the amount of water reaching its roots, the kind of soil in which it grows, and many other factors influence the amount of poison formed.

Another source of variation is the size of the person (or animal) who consumes the poison. As a general rule, the larger the person the more of a poisonous plant must be consumed before symptoms are seen, because there is more body to be poisoned. A small piece of amanita mushroom — no more than a forkful — may be deadly to a small child. An adult must eat four or five times this amount to get a lethal dose. The arrow poisons from the poison tree (*Ackonthera*) of Central Africa may kill a small antelope within a few minutes. The same poisonous arrows may take as long as two days to kill an elephant.

There is also considerable variation in the sensitivity to poison among different species of animals. Locoweed poisoning is a major killer of horses, cattle, and sheep in the western United States. To develop symptoms of locoweed poisoning, cattle must consume more than 2500 pounds of the plant over a three-month period. Horses are more sensitive to locoweed — 600 pounds of the plant eaten over a month and a half are often lethal.

The natural environment is wondrously complicated. Substances move back and forth through all its parts — from air to land, from land to water, and back to the air; they move from plant to animal and from animal to plant. Because the environment is so interconnected, it is not always necessary to come into direct contact with a poisonous plant to show symptoms of poisoning.

For thousands of years there have been reported cases of people being poisoned after eating honey. We now know that there is nothing poisonous about honey itself. Instead, poisonous honey is made by bees that have gathered large amounts of nectar from the flowers of poisonous plants such as rhododendron, buckeye, black locust, or oleander. Sometimes the bees too are poisoned by the nectar. Beekeepers in Nevada have had whole hives of bees killed off after the insects gathered nectar from the flowers of locoweed.

During Colonial times and throughout the eighteenth and nineteenth centuries, parts of America suffered from epidemics of a disease called "milk sickness" or "milk fever." The disease was especially severe in Illinois, Indiana, North Carolina, and Ohio, so severe that in some towns half the people died of the affliction within a few years. President Abraham Lincoln's mother, Nancy Hanks Lincoln, was a victim of milk sickness. Milk sickness took its name from the fact that it was caused by drinking cow's milk. No one understood what the poisonous substance in the milk might be and, because milk was an important part of everybody's diet, the disease was very hard to avoid. Sometimes entire villages were abandoned because farmers could not find a way to prevent their cows from giving poisonous milk. Finally, in the early twentieth century, agricultural researchers established that the disease was caused by a poisonous plant, the white snakeroot. Cattle grazing on snakeroot had been passing the poison along to people through their milk. Today milk sickness is no longer a problem, because farmers are careful not to pasture their cows in fields containing the white snakeroot.

Cows are not the only animals that can carry plant poisons in their milk. If a nursing mother consumes a poisonous plant, there is a possibility that she might pass the poison along to her child through her breast milk. There has been at least one reported case of an infant dying of amanita mushroom poisoning in this manner. The child's mother was completely unaware that she had eaten the poisonous mushroom until long after she had nursed (and thereby poisoned) her baby. The mother too was poisoned, but she did not die.

4

The Plant Kingdom

There are an estimated half-million distinctly different kinds of plants growing throughout the world. This vast number includes such plants as the giant California redwood trees, which may grow hundreds of feet into the air, and tiny one-celled plants so small that they can be seen only with a microscope; it includes wildflowers, ferns, garden vegetables, mosses, mushrooms, and seaweeds. Plants are found almost everywhere — from about two hundred feet beneath the surface of the ocean to more than two miles up the sides of craggy mountains. There are plants growing on the frozen Arctic tundra and in the boiling steam of Yellowstone geysers. There are even tiny plants growing thousands of feet up in the sky, suspended in midair by perpetual winds. Among all these different kinds of plants are all the different kinds of poisonous plants.

But what exactly is a plant? A simple question, perhaps, but like many simple questions, its answer is more complex.

Most plants are able to make their own food, thanks to a

chemical called *chlorophyll*, which is found in their leaves and stems. Chlorophyll gives plants their characteristic green color, and molecules of chlorophyll have the unique ability to capture the energy of sunlight and use it to make a sugar, *glucose*, out of water and carbon dioxide. This process is called *photosynthesis*, from the Greek words *photo* ("light") and *synthesis* ("putting together"). Using the sugar formed by photosynthesis, plus a few minerals from the soil, green plants are able to manufacture everything they need to grow, to reproduce, and, sometimes, to make poisons.

"Something with the ability to carry out photosynthesis" might be a good answer to the question "What is a plant?" except for one fact: all of the fungi (the mushrooms and molds) and most bacteria cannot carry out photosynthesis. In fact, most scientists today agree that the fungi and bacteria are as different from green plants as green plants are from animals. They suggest that instead of two kingdoms — plants and animals — there should be five:

The Kingdom of Animals (*Animalia*)
The Kingdom of Green Plants ("true plants," or *Plantae*)
The Kingdom of Molds and Mushrooms (*Fungi*)
The Kingdom of One-celled Plants and Animals (*Protista*)
The Kingdom of Bacteria and Bluegreen Algae (*Monera*)

This book includes poisonous fungi, bacteria, and bluegreen algae in the category of "plants" because they all seem more like plants than animals. Perhaps the best way to answer "What is a plant?" would be to show how these organisms differ from animals.

One big difference between plants and animals is that most animals can move about freely, while most plants are rooted to the earth. Still, there are many exceptions: sponges, corals, and barnacles are all animals, but they spend their lives anchored in one place on rocks or on the sandy bottom of the sea. On the other hand, many microscopic plants, including the poisonous algae that cause "red tides," are able to swim freely through the water.

Another difference between plants and animals is that animals have nervous systems and plants do not. An animal reacts to changes in its environment through its senses of touch, taste, sight, smell, or hearing, all of which are controlled by nerves. A nervous system allows an animal to react very rapidly. Consider the difference between the ways in which a plant and an animal react to sunlight. If an animal, a person for example, wants to turn toward the sun it needs only to locate the sun with its eyes and move a few muscles — the entire process takes but a second. A plant, on the other hand, must wait while the side of its stem farthest from the sun *grows* ever so slightly more than the side closest to the sun. This causes the stem to turn toward the sun. The process may take hours or even days to complete. Some plants have very rapid reactions. The insect-eating Venus's flytrap can close its leaves around a fly in a matter of seconds; this reaction is not controlled by nerves, however, but by changes in water pressure in the leaves.

It should be mentioned that some people believe that plants are capable of having *feelings* and *emotions*. In a controversial series of experiments, common houseplants were connected to machines called polygraphs (more commonly known as "lie detectors"), which measured subtle changes in electric current flowing through the leaves and stems. Next, the experimenters threatened the plants with injury by holding lighted matches and saying to the plant "I'm going to burn you," or by simply thinking about jabbing the leaves and stems with a sharp pin.

The experimenters reported that these threats caused dramatic changes in the electrical current flowing through the plant, even though the plants were not actually injured.

These experiments have been offered as evidence that plants may somehow be able to think, for how else could they have reacted to the threat? Most scientists believe that it is impossible to think without having a nervous system. Does this mean that plants do, in fact, have nerves? That question cannot yet be answered. One of the biggest difficulties facing this kind of research is that the experiments are very hard to *repeat*. Experiments that worked in one laboratory often times fail to work in another. It is a rule of modern science that before a new experiment is accepted as fact the experiment must be successfully repeated in many different laboratories. Meanwhile, the research goes on. If someday it can be shown that plants truly do have feelings and emotions, it will completely change the science of biology and the way in which people relate to the natural world.

Both plants and animals are made up of small units called *cells*. Some microscopic plants and animals consist of but a single cell, but all of the living things that you can see with your naked eyes are made up of thousands of cells. Your own body consists of about one hundred trillion (100,000,000,000,000) cells. Plant and animal cells are quite different from each other. Every plant cell is surrounded by a rigid "box" called the *cell wall*. Animal cells do not have cell walls. As you might imagine, being encased in a box gives plant cells great strength. A piece of wood is actually billions of plant cells stuck together with a powerful glue that was produced by the tree while it was alive. Plants must sacrifice something for this strength: they cannot move rapidly. Animals are able to move rapidly due to the combination of cells without walls and the presence of a nervous system.

In summary, the major characteristics that distinguish plants from animals are:

1. Green plants, bluegreen algae, and some bacteria are able to carry out photosynthesis.
2. All plants lack a nervous system.
3. All plant cells, including the cells of bacteria, bluegreen algae, and fungi, are surrounded by cell walls.

The poisonous plants fall into three categories: bacteria and bluegreen algae, fungi, and green plants.

BACTERIA AND BLUEGREEN ALGAE

At first glance it is hard to see how bacteria and bluegreen algae could be related. Bacteria are very small, one-celled creatures. Bluegreen algae are much larger; most can be seen with the naked eye. Bacteria are found nearly everywhere — in the air, in water, on the ground, on other plants and animals, and inside the human body. Bacteria are found in the frozen Arctic and in arid deserts. Bluegreen algae, on the other hand, grow only where it is damp, in streams and lakes or on moist rocks. They are called bluegreen because that is their usual color. If you've ever kept fish in a home aquarium, you've probably seen bluegreen algae as a colored scum that forms inside the glass.

The feature that relates bacteria and bluegreen algae is found inside their cells. Within every living cell is a structure called the nucleus. The nucleus may be thought of as the control center of the cell, because inside the nucleus is found the chemical compound called *deoxyribose nucleic acid* (DNA). As discussed earlier, DNA helps control nearly everything that goes on inside the cell: it determines what chemical reactions will take place; it helps determine how large the cell will grow; and it determines what *kind* of cell it will be. The DNA in a bacterial cell contains the exact plan for a particular species of bacteria; the DNA in a frog cell contains all the information needed to make a frog; and inside every one of the cells in your body is a tiny bit of DNA that contains the plan for you.

In all plants and animals *except the bacteria and bluegreen algae,* the nucleus and its DNA are surrounded by a thin sheet of membrane called the *nuclear membrane.* Scientists believe that the very first living cells on earth also lacked a nuclear membrane and, therefore, that the bacteria and bluegreen algae are the living relatives of some of the very first life on earth. The oldest known fossils are of bacteria and bluegreen algae. The very oldest fossil, which appears to be that of a bluegreen alga, was found in South African rocks that are three billion (3,000,000,000) years old. (For comparison, dinosaurs roamed the earth about 100 million years ago.)

Some bacteria and bluegreen algae are poisonous. Bacteria are best known for their ability to cause diseases, among which are bubonic plague, cholera, diphtheria, syphilis, gonorrhea, leprosy, scarlet fever, tetanus, tuberculosis, typhoid fever, whooping cough, pneumonia, dysentery, and strep throat. Most bacteria, however, *do not* cause disease. Billions of harmless bacteria live in our mouths, on our skin, and in our bodies.

Harmful bacteria have two ways of making people sick. Some bacteria actually destroy the cells in our bodies, such as those that cause leprosy, tuberculosis, and the venereal diseases. Others produce poisons that pass into the bloodstream and move about the body, causing such illnesses as diphtheria, tetanus, typhoid fever, and several kinds of food poisoning. The most powerful poison known is produced by the bacterium

Clostridium botulinum, which causes a very serious kind of food poisoning called *botulism*. Many cases of botulism end in death. One ounce of this poison is enough to kill 400 million people.

Most cases of botulism have been traced to improperly canned food that has not been heated enough to kill all the bacteria. Sometimes *Clostridium botulinum* will get into cans through tiny punctures. Almost all known cases of botulism have involved home-canned food, where the only preparation was boiling. For absolute safety, food to be canned must be cooked in a *pressure cooker*. There have been very few cases of botulism due to commercially canned food in the United States, though a few years back a soup manufacturer distributed cans of vichyssoise that were contaminated with *C. botulinum*. As a result, people refused to buy any soups produced by the manufacturer and the company soon went bankrupt. In April 1977 the worst outbreak of botulism poisoning in U.S. history struck the town of Pontiac, Michigan, when more than forty people were poisoned. The disease was traced to home-canned chili peppers that had been served in a local Mexican restaurant.

The most important poisonous bluegreen algae grow in freshwater lakes, ponds, and reservoirs, where the poison may contaminate supplies of drinking water. Most of the time these poisonous algae are no problem because they are present in such small numbers that the poisons they produce are rapidly diluted by the water. But sometimes the algae multiply so rapidly that they cover the entire surface of the pond, coloring the water a pale blue-green. Such rapid growth is called a *bloom*. Under bloom conditions, the level of poison in the water may be high enough to harm animals that drink it. Ducks, geese, cats, dogs, horses, cattle, pigs, sheep, and many other wild and domesticated animals have died after drinking water contaminated with bluegreen algae toxins. There are no recorded cases of human deaths from drinking contaminated waters, but there have been epidemics of severe stomach upset that have been traced to bluegreen algae blooms in reservoirs that supplied drinking water.

The amount of algae that can grow in a lake or a pond is limited by the amounts of phosphorus, nitrogen, and other nutrients present in the water. Normally these amounts are quite low, so the total amount of algae is also low, but if the nutrient level is increased, the algae will begin to grow very rapidly. Sometimes these extra nutrients come from fertilizers that have been washed out of nearby agricultural fields. Sewage is rich in algal nutrients; blooms are often seen in water that has been contaminated with sewage.

The three species of bluegreen algae most commonly found in poisonous blooms are know by the Latin names *Anabaena flosaquae, Aphanizomenon flosaquae,* and *Microcystis aerugnosa.* Although these species have no real common names, biologists sometimes refer to them as "Annie, Fannie, and Mike."

THE FUNGI

The fungi are a very diverse group of plants. In size, they range from the microscopic, one-celled yeasts to the giant "puffballs" that may be more than three feet in diameter and weigh more than fifty pounds. Fungi are found in a wide range of habitats on land and water.

The fungi have been both friends and enemies to human beings. Without the yeasts, we could not make beer or wine, nor could we bake bread, and several kinds of cheese owe their distinctive flavors to the presence of a mold. Many kinds of mushrooms are delicious foods (others, of course, are deadly poisons). Other fungi are the source of medicines. Fungi can also cause diseases in both plants and animals. Fungus damage to agricultural crops costs the average American citizen more than $200 a year in increased food costs. Dry rot, a major form of damage to wooden houses and boats, is caused by fungi.

Of all the fungi, the mushrooms are best known for their poisonous properties, though only about 70 out of the 15,000 existing species are known to cause poisoning in human beings. Even fewer, perhaps not more than half a dozen species, are truly deadly. Mushrooms have earned their lethal reputation because it is so difficult for an amateur to tell the various species apart, and most mushroom gatherers are amateurs. Time after time, the victims of mushroom poisoning will confess from their hospital beds that they thought the mushrooms they had eaten were harmless. All too many mushroom gatherers rely on simple tests to distinguish poisonous from nonpoisonous species. One common belief is that the juice from a poisonous mushroom will cause a silver coin to tarnish. This is completely false! The most poisonous mushroom, the deadly *Amanita*, will not tarnish silver, nor will many other poisonous species. Equally false is the belief that if nonpoisonous mushrooms are gathered at a particular spot, all mushrooms gathered there will be safe, year after year. There is simply no easy test for determining whether or not a mushroom is poisonous. The only way to be sure is to identify the mushroom positively.

Some fungi produce substances that are harmless to people but poisonous to bacteria. These substances are called *antibiotics*. This was first noted in 1928 by the English microbiologist Sir Alexander Fleming. Dr. Fleming had been growing cultures of the bacterium *Staphylococcus aureus*, which causes serious infections in human beings. When the culture plates became accidentally contaminated by mold, Dr. Fleming prepared to destroy and discard the plates, but first he made an important observation: wherever the fungus grew on the plates the bacterium did not. This was an important discovery, because anything that stopped the growth of a disease-causing bacterium was a potentially valuable drug. Through further experiments and much hard work, Dr. Fleming and his colleagues were able to identify the bacteria-killing substance being produced by the fungus. Because the mold was known by the Latin name *Penicillium notatum*, they called the substance penicillin.

As a drug, penicillin has proved to be an extremely valuable contribution to medicine. It is an effective control for the bacteria that cause pneumonia, gas gangrene, diphtheria, spinal meningitis, syphilis, gonorrhea, and several other diseases. Following the discovery of penicillin, scientists began to discover that other molds, as well as several bacteria, also produced anitbiotic substances. Today, millions of people owe their lives to drugs that are really plant-produced poisons.

THE GREEN PLANTS

Most of the living things we call plants are green plants. More than 300,000 distinct species belong to this group. Green plants are the source of all of our food — in fact, they are the source of all the food on the planet. Even if we eat meat, we are feasting on energy that was originally captured by a plant and then passed on to the animal that ate the plant. Nearly all of the oxygen that we breathe has at one time or another passed through green plants. When we burn coal or oil or gasoline, we are using energy that began as sunlight, was stored by a green plant, and then was converted to its present form over millions of years.

SOME IMPORTANT ALKALOIDS, THEIR SOURCES, AND USES

Alkaloid	Plant Source	
	Common Name	*Scientific Name*
Atropine	Belladonna	*Atropa belladonna*
Caffeine	Coffee	*Coffea arabica* and related species
Cocaine	Coca	*Erythroxylun coca*
Coniine	Poison hemlock	*Conium maculatum*
Ergonovine	Ergot	*Claviceps purpurea*
Morphine	Opium poppy	*Papaver somniferum*
Nicotine	Tobacco	*Nicotiniana tabacum*
Quinine	Cinchona	*Cinchona ledgeriana*
Strychnine	—	*Strychnos nux-vomica*
Tubocurarine	Curare	*Chondrodendron tomentosum*

Uses

Used medicinally to dilate the eyes and in the symptomatic treatment of colds and hay fever. Overdoses can be fatal.

As a stimulant, usually in the form of a hot beverage.

Used illegally as a stimulant. Used medicinally as an anesthetic in eye, nose, and throat surgery. Overdoses can be fatal.

Used in the past for various medical purposes. Overdoses can be fatal.

Promotes contraction of smooth muscles and is sometimes used to induce labor in childbirth. Ergot infects wheat and rye, rendering flour made from these plants poisonous. Overdoses can be fatal.

A powerful painkilling drug. Overdoses can be fatal.

Found in smoking tobacco. Concentrated solutions of nicotine are used as insecticides. Overdoses can be fatal.

Used in the cure of malaria.

Powerful poison used to control rats, mice, gophers, etc. At one time it was used as a cathartic drug, but this use has been discontinued. Overdoses can be fatal.

A South American arrow poison. Used medicinally as a muscle relaxant. Overdoses can be fatal.

Green plants give us fibers from which we manufacture paper and cloth; they give us vegetable oils for cooking and lubricating machinery; they are the sources of spices, dyes, and incense. Almost half the drugs used in modern medicine came originally from plants. Most of the world's four billion people survive on diets that are almost exclusively made up of green plants. And almost all of the important poisonous plants are green plants.

The largest subdivision of the green plants is that of the flowering plants, or *angiosperms*. Botanists have identified more than 250,000 species of flowering plants — more than half of all the plants known to man.

Flowering plants were not always the largest group of green plants. In fact, for much of the history of our planet there were no flowering plants at all. The oldest fossils of flowering plants are more than 180 million years old, and while that is quite old, older fossils of all other groups of green plants have been found. When dinosaurs were alive there were very few flowering plants; the plants that covered the land were related more closely to the ferns and to the conifers.

Today flowering plants are the most common land plants in the world. Though there are still great forests of conifers, and ferns and mosses are by no means rare, they are both outnumbered by the flowering plants. Forests of flowering trees spread across the eastern half of North America. The jungles of Asia, Africa, and Central and South America are thick with flowering trees and other flowering plants. The grasses that cover the plains of the American Midwest, of Central Asia and the South African veldt, are flowering plants. Only in the oceans are flowering plants rare (there are only two flowering plants that actually live in the sea, the eelgrasses, *Zostra* and *Phylospadix*).

With so many different flowering plants it is not surprising that there are a great many different kinds of flowers. They come in a wide range of sizes — from flowers too small to be seen with the naked eye to the giant flower of *Raffaelsia*, which measures six feet across. Flowers come in all colors of the rainbow, in black and white, and in all shapes.

A significant proportion of the green plants, perhaps as many as 10 per cent, contain chemicals called *alkaloids*. (Alkaloids are also present in some fungi and, very rarely, in animals.) Alkaloid means "like an alkali," a reference to the chemical properties of these compounds. Alkaloids, like alkalis, have a bitter, unpleasant taste, and, again like alkalis, they are able to react with acids to form salts. Alkaloids are composed almost entirely of the elements carbon, hydrogen, and nitrogen. Many alkaloids have powerful effects on animal metabolism, especially on the functioning of the nervous system. A surprisingly large proportion of the poisonous green plants owe their toxic properties to the presence of alkaloids. Many of the medicines that have been derived from plants are alkaloids. On page 44 are listed some of the more important alkaloids, their properties, and the kinds of plants that produce them.

In the second part of this book, we will examine some of these plants, and many others, in more detail.

PART TWO

5

Poisonous Plants
in the United States

The 1974 *figures* for accidental plant ingestion (swallowing) by human beings in the United States mention 150 different plants (not including mushrooms or algae) plus a large number of plants that were "unclassified." As mentioned earlier, many of these plants are not really poisonous but were reported to the Poison Control Centers in the concern that they might be. Of those plants that can be dangerous, the top twenty-five reported to Poison Control Centers are listed in the table on page 52.

Though many of the plants in this list can be deadly, they very rarely are. Of the 11,097 cases of plant ingestion reported during 1974, 1187 showed definite symptoms of poisoning, 260 required hospitalization, and only 1 died. Many more people actually went to the hospital (and many more died) as the result of eating a poisonous plant, but these cases never found their way into the official statistics. Most of these cases were not reported because the doctors already knew the names of the plants concerned and did not have to contact the Poison Control

THE TWENTY-FIVE MOST FREQUENTLY MENTIONED POISONOUS PLANTS

From 1974 National Clearinghouse for Poison Control Centers Reports

Rank	Common Name	Scientific Name
1	Philodendron	Several different members of the Arum family (Araceae), including *Philodendron*
2	Yew	Various species of *Taxus*
3	Woody nightshade (Bittersweet)	*Solanum dulcamara* (red berries) or *Solanum nigrum* (black or purple berries)
4	Marijuana	*Cannabis sativa*

Location	Poisonous Parts	Symptoms
Natives of tropical regions of the world. Grown as houseplants in the U.S. (outdoors in the South and in Hawaii).	Leaves	Causes a burning sensation in the mouth. In extreme cases the mouth and tongue become so swollen that victims choke to death.
See page 88	See page 88	See page 88
S. *dulcamara* comes from Europe, but grows in woods in parts of North America. S. *nigrum* is a native plant of the eastern U.S.	Leaves, roots, and berries	Burning in the throat, nausea, dizziness, dilated pupils, weakness, convulsions. Can be fatal.
Native of Eurasia, but grown throughout the world. Most commonly seen as the dried leaves or flowers, which are smoked for their hallucinogenic effect.	Leaves, flowers	In moderate amounts, marijuana produces a mild, pleasant intoxication. Overdoses produce nausea, poor coordination, and, rarely, coma.

Rank	Common Name	Scientific Name
5	Holly	Various species of *Ilex*
6	Poinsettia	*Euphorbia pulcherrima*
7	Dieffenbachia, Dumbcane	Various species of *Dieffenbachia*
8	Black elderberry	*Sambucus canadensis*
9	Oleander	*Nerium oleander*
10	Acorns (oak)	Various species of *Quercus*
11	Jerusalem cherry	*Solanum pseudocapsicum*
12	Elephant ears	*Calocasia antiquoram, C. esculenta*

Location	Poisonous Parts	Symptoms
Mostly grown as ornamental foliage that is displayed at Christmastime.	Berries	A large number of berries (probably more than twenty) may cause vomiting and diarrhea.
A house plant, often displayed at Christmastime. Grows outdoors in the southern U.S. and Hawaii.	Leaves and stems	Stomach upset.
A native of tropical America, grown as a house plant.	Leaves	Same as philodendron.
A native plant, growing from Canada south to Florida and west to Arizona.	Roots, stems, leaves, and *unripe* berries; ripe berries are edible	Nausea, vomiting, diarrhea.
See page 112	See page 112	See page 112
Throughout the U.S. and Canada.	Acorns	A very large number may cause damage to the digestive tract, but this is rare. Acorns have a bitter, unpleasant taste.
A house plant. Grows wild in Hawaii.	Berries	Same as woody nightshade.
House plants in most of the U.S. Grown outdoors in Florida and Hawaii.	Leaves	Same as philodendron.

Rank	Common Name	Scientific Name
13	Jimsonweed	*Datura stramonium*
14	Pokeweed, Pokeberries	*Phytolacca americana*
15	Peyote	*Lophophora williamsii*
16	Castor bean	*Ricinus communis*
17	Mistletoe	*Phoradendron villosum, P. flavescens*
18	Buckeye, Horsechestnut	Various species of *Aesculus*
19	Iris	Various species of *Iris*

Location	Poisonous Parts	Symptoms
See page 138	See page 138	See page 138
	Roots, shoots, and berries	Nausea, vomiting, blurred vision. Large amounts can cause death by respiratory failure.
A small cactus, growing wild in Texas and Mexico, eaten for its hallucinogenic effects.	The entire plant	Peyote is a moderately strong hallucinogenic plant. Side effects include nausea, headache, vomiting.
See page 141	See page 141	See page 141
P. villosum is a parasite on oak trees in the western U.S. P. flavescens is a parasite on trees in the southern U.S. Both are displayed in houses during Christmastime.	Leaves and berries	Stomach upset. In very severe cases, death has came from failure to breathe.
Buckeye grows throughout the U.S.	Leaves, flowers, sprouts, and seeds	Vomiting, diarrhea, lack of coordination, paralysis. California Indians used extract of buckeye as a fish poison.
Wild and cultivated irises are found throughout the U.S.	Leaves, roots	Severe stomach upset, sometimes accompanied by burning in the mouth.

Rank	Common Name	Scientific Name
20	Privet	*Ligustrum vulgare*
21	Rhubarb	*Rheum rhaponticum*
22	Lily of the valley	*Convallaria majalis*
23	Rhododendron, Laurel, Azalea	Various species of *Rhododendron*
24	English Ivy	*Hedera helix*
25	Lantana	*Lantana camara*

Location	Poisonous Parts	Symptoms
A native of Europe; grown throughout the U.S. as a hedge plant.	Leaves, stems	Vomiting, diarrhea, digestive upset.
In vegetable gardens and grocery stores.	Leaves	Stomach pain, nausea, vomiting. In severe cases, convulsions, internal bleeding, coma, and death.
Native of Eurasia; grown in flower gardens throughout the U.S., and sometimes found in the wild.	Roots, leaves, flowers, and fruit	Similar to *Digitalis* poison (see page 144).
Some are natives, others are introduced from Asia. Grown in flower gardens throughout the U.S.	The whole plant	Vomiting, weakness, and, in extreme cases, paralysis and death.
See page 114	See page 114	'See page 114
A native of the southern U.S., now grown in gardens throughout the country.	Berries	Stomach upset, weakness, and, very rarely, death from failure to breathe.

Centers for help. And it is only when someone calls on a center (usually by telephone) for help that a case is recorded.

Most of the plants in the top twenty-five are not on the list because of their unusually strong poisons, but rather because they are very common plants and therefore more likely to be eaten by young children.

In *Human Poisoning from Native and Cultivated Plants*, James Hardin and Jay Arena have compiled this list of the plants that are responsible for the overwhelming majority of accidental poisonings:

WILD PLANTS

Skin Rash from Touching the Plant

Manchineel	Poisonwood	Wild parsnip
Poison ivy	Spotted spurge	Woodnettle
Poison oak	Spurge nettle	
Poison sumac	Trumpet creeper	

Poisonous When Eaten

Apple-of-Peru	Chinaberry	Holly
Baneberry	Coontie	Horse nettle
Beech	Corn cockel	Hydrangea
Black cherry	Coyotillo	Jack-in-the-pulpit
Black locust	Cycads	Jequirity pea
Black snakeroot	Dicentra	Jimsonweed
Bloodroot	Dogbane	Kentucky coffee tree
Blue cohosh	Elderberry	Larkspur
Buckeye	Elephant ear	Lobelia
Buckthorn	False hellebore	Mayapple
Burning bush	Golden seal	Mescal bean
Buttercup	Ground cherry	Mexican pricklepoppy

Mistletoe
Monkshood
Moonseed
Mountain laurel
Mulberry
Mushrooms
Nightshade
Oak (acorns)
Poison hemlock

Pokeweed
Prickly poppy
Rattlebox
Rayless goldenrod
Rhododendron
Rock poppy
Spurge
Star-of-Bethlehem
Strawberry bush

Virginia creeper
Water hemlock
White snakeroot
Wild balsam apple
Yellow jessamine
Yellow nightshade
Yew

CULTIVATED PLANTS OF THE YARD AND GARDEN

Skin Rash

Gas plant

Poisonous When Eaten

Akee
Amaryllis
Anemone
Angel's trumpet
Arnica
Autumn crocus
Azalea
Belladonna
Betel nut
Bird-of-paradise
Bittersweet
Black henbane
Bleeding heart
Boxwood
Burning bush
Caladium
Caper spurge

Cassava
Castor bean
Cestrum
Cherry
Chinaberry
Christmas rose
Clematis
Coca
Crape jasmine
Crownflower
Crown-of-thorns
Cycads
Cypress spurge
Daphne
Devil's trumpet
Dieffenbachia
Duranta

English ivy
Fave bean
Finger cherry
Four-o'clock
Foxglove
Glory lily
Golden chain
Hill gooseberry
Holly
Horsechestnut
Hyacinth
Hyacinth bean
Hydrangea
Jessamine
Jerusalem cherry
Jetbead
Kentucky coffee tree

Lantana
Larkspur
Laurel
Lignum vitae
Lily-of-the-valley
Mescal bean
Monkshood
Morning glory
  (seeds)
Mustard
Narcissus
Ochrosia plum
Oleander
Pencil tree

Physic nut
Poinciana
Pongam
Prickly poppy
Privet
Purge nut
Rattlebox
Rhododendron
Rhubarb
Rubber vine
Sandbox tree
Snow-on-the-
  mountain
Spring adonis

Spurge
Star-of-Bethlehem
Sweet pea
Tobacco
Tomato
Trumpet flower
Tung oil tree
Wisteria
Yellow allamanda
Yellow jessamine
Yellow oleander
Yew

HOUSE PLANTS

Amaryllis
Bird-of-paradise
Crown-of-thorns
Dieffenbachia

Glory lily
Hyacinth
Narcissus
Pencil tree

Philodendron
Poinsettia

CHRISTMAS GREENERY

Boxwood
English ivy
European bittersweet

Holly
Jequirity pea
Jerusalem cherry
Mistletoe

Mountain laurel
Poinsettia
Yew

On the following pages you will find the stories and descriptions of some of the more important and interesting poisonous plants found in the United States. Not all of these plants are native to North America, but all of them are found in some or all of the fifty states.

THE FUNGI

Ergot

Other Common Name: None

Scientific Name: *Claviceps purpurea*

Description: The poisonous stage of the ergot fungus's life cycle is a hard, dark structure called a *sclerotium*, which infects and replaces the seeds of cereals and wild grasses.

Location: Ergot grows on several species of wild grass and on rye, wheat, barley, and other cereals. The fungus is found in the United States, Canada, and Europe.

How It Poisons: Animals may be poisoned from grazing on infected wild grasses. Humans are poisoned from eating bread baked from flour that is made from ergotty grain. The poisonous substances in ergot are alkaloids that are chemically related to *lysergic acid*. The major toxic effect is strong contractions of smooth muscles.

During the Middle Ages, many parts of Europe suffered epidemics of a terrible disease known as Saint Anthony's Fire.

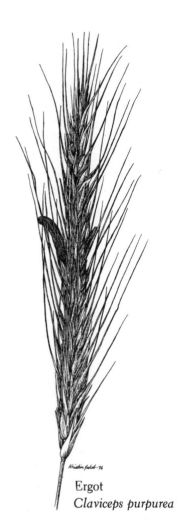

Ergot
Claviceps purpurea

Two of the very worst epidemics occurred in France during the years 944 and 1090, when tens of thousands of men, women, and children died.

It is widely believed that the victims of Saint Anthony's Fire had been possessed by the Devil, and it is easy to understand why: the poor victims often screamed that they were burning while their bodies were seized by violent convulsions. Often they cried out in terror that they were being attacked by wild animals or horrible monsters. In some cases, their hands, feet, and ears would turn black as though charred by a fire, and pieces of flesh would slough off. If the victim was a pregnant woman, she would almost always lose her unborn baby through a miscarriage.

The doctors of those times could do very little to ease their patients' suffering. If they could, the victims would make a pilgrimage to the shrine of Saint Anthony in Egypt, for it was thought that Saint Anthony had special powers for driving out demons.

In fact, the disease was *not* caused by the Devil; it was caused by ordinary bread or, to be more precise, by something in the bread, but this was not discovered until hundreds of years later.

In 1597, a group of French physicians announced that Saint Anthony's Fire was actually a disease caused by certain rye plants that produced peculiar, black, swollen, poisonous grains. When this grain was ground into flour and then baked into rye bread, the bread too became poisonous. The poisonous grain was very easy to identify and was usually thrown away before it could be made into flour. But when the harvest was poor and food was scarce, all of the rye grown would be used as food regardless of its condition. Then the worst epidemics would occur.

The French doctors thought that the swollen rye grain looked very much like the hind claws of a rooster — a cock's spur — so they called the poisonous grain *ergot*, the French word for "spur." Within a few years, doctors discovered that the black, swollen "grains" were not really grains at all but the spore sacs of a fungus that had eaten away the real grain and had assumed its shape. Today, we call the fungus ergot and refer to the diseased grain as being ergotty.

Rye is not the only plant that can become ergotty. Wheat and barley, as well as many wild grasses, may also be infected by the ergot fungus. Nor is the fungus confined to Europe; it has been found throughout the continental United States and much of Canada.

The poisons produced by ergot are powerful alkaloids whose major effect on human beings and animals is to cause their *smooth muscles* to contract. In serious cases of ergot poisoning, the smooth muscles of the blood vessels may become so tightly contracted that no blood can flow into them. Deprived of a fresh supply of blood, the hands and feet will blacken and die, a condition called *gangrene*. Ergot may cause the muscles of a pregnant woman's uterus to contract so violently that the unborn child will be forced out before it is large enough to survive outside its mother.

Ergot poisoning in human beings is rare today. In the United States and in many other countries, harvested grains are carefully inspected for dangerous amounts of ergot. The last known epidemic of ergot poisoning struck the small French town of Pont Saint-Esprit in 1951. But not long ago, a tragedy was narrowly avoided in the small town of Sand Point, Washington, where a church group had purchased ten thousand pounds of ergotty grain direct from a grain company. The group planned to grind the grain into flour and distribute it to church members. The miller became suspicious when he noticed dark spots on the grain and in the resulting flour. He called a local agricultural inspector, who identified the spots as ergot, quite enough of the fungus to make many loaves of deadly bread.

Although the risk to human beings has been reduced, ergot poisoning of animals remains a serious problem. Often, grain that is too ergotty to be used for flour will be sold as livestock or chicken feed. Cattle that eat large amounts of ergotty grain exhibit many of the same symptoms that people do: they suffer convulsions, miscarriages, and gangrene. There are many veterinarians in the United States who feel that the present laws regulating the ergot content of grain are not strict enough. They believe that if grain is not fit for human consumption it is also unfit for animals and should be destroyed. Wild grasses may sometimes be infected with ergot, posing a danger to grazing animals.

Like many other poisonous plants, the ergot fungus is also the source of valuable medicines. One of the chemicals produced by the fungus, the alkaloid ergonovine, is sometimes given to women to help control the bleeding that sometimes follows childbirth. Small amounts of ergonovine have also been used to treat migraine headaches. Lysergic acid, another chemical produced by the fungus, is used to manufacture the powerful drug *lysergic acid diethylamide*, better known as LSD. There are some doctors who believe that LSD may be a valuable drug for helping people "expand their consciousness" and thereby solve their emotional problems. But there are many more doctors who believe that LSD is extremely dangerous and that instead of helping people solve problems it creates new ones. One thing is sure: the possession and use of LSD is illegal in the United States and in many other countries.

The Mushrooms

For most of their lives, the plants that we call mushrooms (or toadstools) look nothing at all like mushrooms. In fact, most of the time they can't even be seen by the naked eye. Only for a few days out of the year do these fungi appear as mushrooms. The rest of the time they exist as a mass of tiny, white threads growing silently in soil or rotting wood.

These threads, called *hyphae* (hy-fee), may consist of thousands of cells. The entire mass of hyphae is called a *mycelium*; it may extend through the soil for a hundred feet or more. As it grows, the mycelium produces chemicals that dissolve any organic matter it touches. This dissolved organic matter is the fungus's food, so when a fungus causes wood to rot, it is actually eating the wood.

At certain times of the year — when the ground is damp and the air is warm — the mycelium begins to grow very rapidly and the hyphae actually weave themselves into mushrooms. Mushrooms can appear overnight, pushing up through lawns, piles of dead leaves, and even through solid concrete. They disappear nearly as fast as they appear. The inky cap mushroom (*Coprinus*) dissolves into a black, gooey mass within a few days, and few mushrooms survive more than a week or two.

The mushroom is actually the "fruit" of the fungus, because, like the fruit of a flowering plant, a mushroom is a reproductive organ. To be more precise, a mushroom is a sex organ, a structure in which sexual reproduction takes place. The actual sexual reproduction takes place on the gills of the mushroom, the thin sheets of tissue on the lower surface of the mushroom's cap.

Sexual reproduction in the mushroom is somewhat different from that in human beings. In human reproduction, a male and a female sex cell come together to form a single cell called a *zygote*. The zygote then develops by growing and dividing millions of times until it has formed a new human being. Mushrooms have no male and female sex cells. Instead, each cell in the mycelium contains two nuclei. These pairs of nuclei come together in the gills to form a zygote, which then divides to produce two or four spores. When these spores drop to the ground they grow into new mycelia. A single mushroom produces an enormous number of spores — several billion.

The color of the spores is a valuable clue in identifying mushrooms. It is not always possible to tell the color of the spores by looking at the gills, for they may be either darker or lighter than the spores they produce. To determine the actual color, a mushroom hunter makes what is called a *spore print*. Making a spore print is not hard and, as you will see, it is one way of making sure that you never eat a deadly mushroom. Make your own spore prints by following these steps:

1. Cut the stalk off a mushroom as close to the cap as possible. If you can't find a wild mushroom, use a large fresh mushroom from the grocery store. Canned or dried mushrooms will *not* give spore prints.

2. Take a sheet of black paper and a sheet of white paper and lay them side by side on a flat surface.

3. Place the mushroom cap on the papers with the gill side *down*. Half the cap should be over the black paper and half over the white.

4. Cover the mushroom cap with a glass or glass bowl turned upside down.

5. Wait for about two hours; remove the glass and lift the mushroom cap. The mushroom's spores will have left a pattern on the paper. If the spores are light-colored they will be best seen against the black background. If they are dark, they can best be seen on the white paper.

Almost all deaths from mushroom poisoning are caused by the genus *Amanita*. ALL AMANITAS HAVE WHITE SPORES. Therefore, even if a mushroom hunter knows nothing else, he or she can be almost certain of never eating a deadly mushroom by simply never eating a mushroom that has white spores. There are, of course, several poisonous (but not deadly) mushrooms with dark spores and many edible mushrooms with light spores.

By the way, if you made a spore print using a mushroom from the grocery store, you should have gotten a purple-brown print. This color is characteristic of *Agaricus bisporus*, the commercially grown meadow mushroom.

Poisonous mushrooms — or toadstools, if you prefer — range in their effects from a mild stomach upset to a slow and painful death. Sometimes the names of the mushrooms offer clues to their effects. For example, *Russula emetica* means "the *Russula* that causes vomiting." *Amanita virosa* means "poisonous amanita."

Several of the poisonous fungi contain chemicals that have powerful effects on the mind. These chemicals can produce bizarre hallucinations and visions of brilliant, dancing colors. In Mexico and Central America the Aztec Indians used mind-altering mushrooms in their religious rituals. The Aztecs called these mushrooms *teonanacatl*, which means "God's flesh." The Aztecs believed that when they ate these mushrooms they became closer to God and could actually see the future. When the Spaniards conquered Mexico, their priests tried to discourage the religious use of mushrooms, calling it a pagan practice.

Although the Spanish conquerors succeeded in destroying much of the Indian culture that they had found in the New World, they were unable to eliminate the use of the *teonanacatl* mushrooms. During the 1950s, an American banker and explorer, R. Gordon Wasson, journeyed into isolated Mexican mountain villages searching for Indian tribes that might still be using these "magic mushrooms." High in the mountains of the state of Oaxaca (wah-*ha*-ka), Wasson found that the use of these mushrooms in religious rituals was still flourishing among the Mazatec tribe. Still later he found several other tribes that used mushrooms in their ceremonies. Most of these mushrooms, Wasson found, belonged to the genus *Psilocybe* (sill-*oss*-a-bee). He himself ate some of these mushrooms and found their taste awful — like "rancid grease" — but he found the visions beautiful and the entire experience both joyous and profoundly moving.

Deadly Amanita Mushroom

Other Common Names: Death Angel, Destroying Angel, Death Cup

Scientific Name: *Amanita phalloides* (also A. *verna*, A. *virosa*, and A. *bisporiger*)

Description: "Deadly amanita" refers to more than one species, but all have in common:

> 1. White spores.
> 2. Large size: eight or more inches high, with caps several inches across.
> 3. A ring (*annulus*), a thin strip of tissue hanging from the stalk and surrounding it.
> 4. A bulbous base (*volva*) on the stalk. Often, the volva separates from the stalk to form a "cup."

Location: In almost every state, in all Canadian provinces, and throughout Europe. Its usual habitat is woodlands, but it is very occasionally found in pastures and grasslands.

How It Poisons: The deadly amanita is the *most* poisonous mushroom. Even a portion of one mushroom is enough to kill an adult, and no more than a forkful can be fatal to a child. The mushroom produces two poisons, *amanitin* and *phalloidin*, of which phalloidin is the most poisonous. Amanita poisons attack the liver and kidneys, and death comes from liver failure. The first symptoms are noticed from eight to twenty-

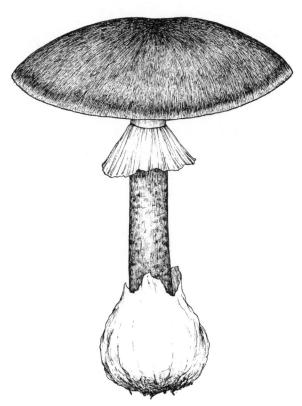

Amanita phalloides

four hours (the average is twelve hours) after eating the mushroom. More than half of all cases of deadly amanita poisoning end in death.

There are several different species of deadly amanita growing in the United States and Canada, but even mushroom experts do not agree on the scientific names for all of them. But all of these mushrooms look very much alike, and all of them are very poisonous. Some of the deadly amanitas are pure white; these are commonly called "destroying angels." Other deadly amanitas are darker, usually with greenish brown caps. *Amanita phalloides* has a greenish brown cap. If you spend much time in the country out of doors, you will probably see amanitas because they are common mushrooms.

Until very recently there was little that doctors could do to help victims of the deadly amanitas. The first symptoms of amanita poisoning do not even appear until eight to twelve hours after the mushroom has been eaten and most of it has been digested. At first the victim suffers from horrible stomach pains, vomiting, and diarrhea. Later the pain may cease and the victim may begin to feel better. This recovery is deceptive, for it is followed by a rapid failure of the liver and kidneys. The victim slips into a deep coma and dies, usually from liver damage.

During the early 1950s, doctors in Czechoslovakia began experimenting with a new drug called *thioctic acid*. Since it was known to protect the liver against the actions of other poisons, the Czech doctors wanted to see if it could also protect against the deadly amanitas. Their results were encouraging. Several victims of *Amanita phalloides* were saved from almost certain death. Further tests of thioctic acid in Germany and Italy also produced positive results, and many more lives were saved.

It is fitting that the drug was developed in Europe, because mushroom gathering is much more popular (and mushroom poisoning more common) there than in the United States.

Thioctic acid got its first test in the United States in 1970, when it saved the life of a New Jersey man who had eaten a stew containing one of the white amanitas. Doctors at San Francisco General Hospital have since used thioctic acid to save the lives of two California mushroom gathers who ate *Amanita phalloides*.

Thioctic acid is a valuable drug, but it is not one hundred per cent effective. Some victims of amanita poisoning will die no matter what is done for them. The conclusion is simple: anyone who plans to eat wild mushrooms should learn how to identify the amanitas and then avoid them.

The Fly Mushroom

Other Common Name: Fly agaric

Scientific Name: *Amanita muscaria*

Description: A large mushroom with a cap three to eight inches across. The cap is most commonly yellow or orange-red, speckled with small white "crumbs." Like the deadly amanita, the fly mushroom has white spores, a ring around the stalk, and a volva at the base (but no "cup").

Location: Throughout the United States, Europe, and Asia, usually growing in woods (especially pine woods).

How It Poisons: The principal poisonous substance is *muscarine*. The first symptoms of poisoning are usually noticed within three hours of eating the mushroom (often sooner). Symptoms include blurred vision, sweating, lowered blood pressure, an abnormally slow heartbeat, stomach pain, and difficulty in breathing. Death is rare, but if it occurs the cause is failure to breathe.

The fly mushroom gets its name from the fact that it is frequently surrounded by dead flies. Apparently the mushroom is attractive to flies, who nibble on the cap and die of poisoning. Although it is closely related to the deadly amanita, the fly

Kristin Jakob - 76

Amanita muscaria

mushroom produces a different kind of poison, *muscarine*, that is not nearly as lethal and takes effect much more rapidly.

The symptoms of muscarine poisoning are almost exactly the opposite of the symptoms of atropine poisoning, which is caused by the poisonous nightshades. Muscarine causes the pupils of the eye to contract, atropine makes them dilate; muscarine causes the stomach muscles to contract, atropine relaxes them; muscarine slows the heartbeat, atropine speeds it. For this reason, doctors often use atrophine as an antidote to muscarine poisoning — one plant poison is used to treat another.

The fly mushroom may be the solution to a riddle that has puzzled botanists for many years. In the *Rig Veda*, an ancient holy book of the Hindu religion, there are many passages that tell of a marvelous plant called *soma*. When soma is eaten it is supposed to give glorious visions. One passage says that soma will take a person "beyond earth and sky." Nowhere in the *Rig Veda* is there a description of what soma looks like, so botanists have advanced many theories about what it might be, including, recently, that soma is the fly mushroom.

This theory comes from R. Gordon Wasson, the same explorer who journeyed into the Mexican mountains in search of the *teonanacatl* mushroom. Wasson observed that the fly mushroom has been used as an intoxicating drug by the Tartar tribes of Siberia. These tribesmen had a practice that most people would find thoroughly disgusting: they collected the urine of people who had eaten the fly mushroom and then gave it to other people to drink. Drinking the urine produced the same intoxication that resulted from eating the mushroom. Wasson believes that some of the passages in the *Rig Veda* describe this same practice of drinking urine and that this is strong evidence that soma is actually *Amanita muscaria*.

Whatever the truth about soma, it is clear that the fly mushroom is a very, very dangerous intoxicating drug. And while it may produce intoxication, it can also make a person horribly ill, sometimes leading to death.

Inky Cap Mushroom

Other Common Name: None

Scientific Name: *Coprinus atramentarius* (there are many other species known as "inky caps," and many are not poisonous)

Description: This mushroom stands two to four inches high with a grayish brown cap that is one to three inches across. A few days after the mushroom sprouts from the ground, the cap begins to dissolve into an inky, black liquid, hence its common name.

Location: Europe and the United States.

How It Poisons: This small mushroom is not very poisonous. In fact, many mushroom identification books state flatly that it is edible, and for most people it is. But for a very few people, and only under special circumstances, it is a poisonous plant. Why this is, we do not know.

To be poisonous, this mushroom must be eaten with alcoholic beverages such as beer, wine, or whiskey. In certain people, the mushroom will cause their face and other parts of their bodies to turn a deep purple-red. This color fades quickly — within an hour or two — but it may return later if more alcohol is consumed. The symptoms do not last for more than a day and they produce no permanent damage.

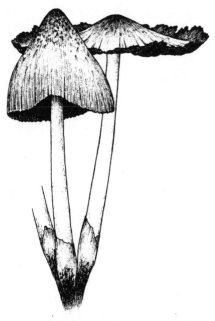

Coprinus atramentarius

ALGAE

Red Tides

Other Common Names: Poison tides

Scientific Name: Paralytic poisons, the most dangerous to human beings, are produced by several species in the genus *Gonyaulax*.

Description: See the photograph opposite.

Location: In all the world's oceans. Poisonous species of *Gonyaulax* are found along the New England coast and the coasts of California, Oregon, Washington, British Columbia, and Alaska.

How They Poison: Human beings are poisoned by eating shellfish that have concentrated large numbers of poisonous dinoflagellates, several species of one-celled plants, in their tissues. The poisons in *Gonyaulax* act on the nerves, causing paralysis. Death, if it occurs, is from failure to breathe.

In the middle of September 1972 a large number of dead birds were found floating in the estuary of the Merrimack River at

Gonyaulax excavata, the one-celled plant responsible for the 1972 Massachusetts Red Tide, here magnified 5200 times.

Plum Island, Massachusetts. At first fish and game authorities thought that the birds had been killed by insecticides that had been sprayed on nearby farmlands, but when they were studied at the state health laboratory, scientists found instead that the birds' stomachs were filled with broken bits of clam and mussel shells.

At the same time, about twenty miles to the south in Gloucester, scientists at the University of Massachusetts Marine Biology Laboratory observed a reddish brown mass floating in the harbor. After examining this substance under a microscope and performing chemical tests, the marine biologists determined that it was made up of billions and billions of microscopic poisonous plants. Further investigations revealed that these reddish brown clumps were drifting all along the coastline. Massachusetts was experiencing a large outbreak of what is called "the red tide."

The plants that caused the red tide are called *dinoflagellates*. Each dinoflagellate consists of a single cell so small that it can only be seen through a microscope. Dinoflagellate means "rotating flagellate," which refers to the way these little plants move, with a tumbling, spinning motion. Dinoflagellates can move because each cell has two thin whips called *flagellae* (fla-*jel*-ly), which beat against the water like the oars of a rowboat.

Dinoflagellates are found in all the oceans of the world. Dinoflagellates are eaten by tiny animals, who in turn are eaten by still larger animals, and so on up the food chain. Together with another group of one-celled plants — the diatoms — dinoflagellates are the source of most of the food in the seas.

Dinoflagellates are not usually present in large enough numbers to cause red tide. In fact, scientists really do not know why red tides occur. Some scientists think that red tides are triggered by increases in temperature and in the amount of sunlight that falls on the water, since most red tides develop during the summer months. But red tides have also developed during the winter. Other scientists have suggested that red tides start when high levels of nutrients collect in the water, causing dinoflagellate growth to speed up in the same way that fertilizer speeds the growth of garden vegetables. But again this is not always true. Along the California coast, for example, red tides can occur when nutrient levels are at their lowest. If heat, light, and nutrients were the most important factors causing red tides, one would expect that all other plants in the sea would also grow rapidly during the time of a red tide, and this does not happen. The distinguishing feature of a red tide is that it contains enormous numbers of plants, *all of a single species.*

Whatever the reasons for a red tide, if one does occur, and if it is made up of a poisonous species of dinoflagellate, there can be trouble.

When news of the poisonous red tide reached the Massachusetts Department of Public Health, action was swift. The governor immediately declared a public health emergency and banned the taking or selling of shellfish in the state. At the same time, public health workers made sure that no markets were selling shellfish that had been taken from any of the waters touched by the red tide. Why was so much attention being directed toward shellfish? Because the biggest danger is that people will eat shellfish that have been contaminated by poisonous dinoflagellates. Clams, mussels, scallops, and other shellfish are continuously pumping water across their gills, straining from it the tiny plants and animals that they eat. During a red tide, shellfish strain out the poisonous dinoflagellates and the poison becomes concentrated in the shellfish meat. People who eat enough of this meat can be poisoned.

Along the New England coast, and on the West Coast from California to Alaska, red tides are caused by dinoflagellates of the genus *Gonyaulax*. Poisonous species of *Gonyaulax* produce a nerve poison that acts very much like curare (see page 154) and, pound for pound, is actually much stronger. The first symptoms of poisoning develop some fifteen minutes to five hours after contaminated shellfish is eaten. At first the victims feel a tingling sensation in their hands and feet. Later, if enough poison was consumed, the victims may be completely paralyzed. In cases of complete paralysis, the victims may die because they are unable to breathe. However, if they can survive the first twelve hours or so, they will usually recover completely in about one day.

People were lucky during the 1972 Massachusetts red tide, since it was discovered early enough. Very few people ate poisoned shellfish (there were twenty-six cases in all), and none of them died. Yet people have not always been so lucky. Along the coast of Alaska there is a body of water called Peril Strait, which gets its name from something that happened many years ago. In 1799 a party of Russian explorers and their Indian guides camped on a beach along the coast of Alaska. The entire group feasted on mussels that they had pried from nearby rocks. They did not know that the mussels had been contaminated by a poisonous tide, and as a result, more than one hundred men died.

Not all red tides are poisonous, and not all poisonous tides are red. Sometimes sea water contains enough poisonous dinoflagellates to contaminate shellfish thoroughly and yet not enough to change the color of the water. Since this condition develops most often during the summer, many areas that experience poisonous tides may automatically quarantine shellfish for the summer.

In the Gulf of Mexico poisonous tides often have an oily yellow color. The dinoflagellates that cause this "yellow tide" have a different kind of poison from that of *Gonyaulax*. This poison is not concentrated in shellfish, so it is not as great a threat to human beings, but it can kill fish and other sea animals. In 1948 a severe outbreak of this yellow tide hit the west coast of Florida. The water contained so many poisonous dinoflagellates that the spray from the surf irritated the skin of people walking along the beaches.

The Old Testament book of Exodus records the story of how God sent a series of plagues against the Egyptians so that they would free the Jews from slavery. One of these plagues sounds very much like a red tide: "All the waters that were in the river were turned to blood. And the fish that was in the river died; and the river stank, and the Egyptians could not drink of the water of the river . . ." If this "blood" in the River Nile was really a red tide, it must have been a very rare event, because never in the past three thousand years has anyone seen a red tide on the Nile.

GYMNOSPERMS

Yew

Other Common Name: Ground hemlock (not to be confused with the other poisonous hemlocks, which are flowering plants)

Scientific Name: Various species of *Taxus*

Description: The yews are evergreen trees and shrubs with flat, pointed, needlelike leaves. In the United States the most common species are the Japanese yew and the English yew, which are both shrubs that are commonly planted in gardens. The Western yew, a tree, and the Canadian yew, a shrub, are the most common wild species. Yews belong to a large group of plants called the *gymnosperms* (*jim*-no-sperms), which include the pine, fir, spruce, and redwood trees. Gymnosperms are related by the fact that they produce seeds but not flowers.

Location: Throughout the United States. Most cases of accidental poisoning are caused by cultivated species, especially the Japanese yew (*Taxus cuspidata*) and the English yew (*Taxus baccata*).

How they poison: Very few gymnosperms are poisonous, but the yew makes up for this by being *very* poisonous. All parts of the yew contain the poisonous alkaloid *taxine*. Animals are

Yew
Taxus baccata

sometimes killed from eating the bark, leaves, or seeds. People are most often poisoned by the fruit of the yew tree. The fruit of the yew develops at the tip of each branch. Each fruit consists of a single seed surrounded by a fleshy pink or red "cup" called an *aril*. To a young child, the fruit of the yew may look like a delicious berry. If children eat enough of these berries they can get very sick, but luckily the fruit is the least poisonous part of the plant, so death from yew poisoning is *very* rare.

For thousands of years the wood of the yew tree has been prized for making archers' bows. The legendary archer Robin Hood is said to have used a yew bow. The yew's scientific name, *Taxus*, comes from the ancient word *toxon*, which means "bow." You may remember that the word *toxin*, meaning "poison," comes from the same Greek word.

FLOWERING PLANTS

Poison Oak and Poison Ivy

Other Common Names: None

Scientific Names: Poison ivy, *Rhus radicans*; poison oak, *Rhus diversiloba*

Description: Poison oak and poison ivy look very much alike. (Even the professional botanist sometimes has trouble telling them apart.) Both occur most commonly as woody shrubs from three to ten feet tall, but it is not unusual to find them growing as stout vines that can climb twenty feet up the side of a tree (or a house!).

Each leaf of poison oak or poison ivy consists of three leaflets. A common saying that may help you to avoid these troublesome plants is "Leaflets three: let it be!" The shapes and the colors of these leaflets are highly variable. The leaflets of both plants may have their edges lobed or smooth. During much of the spring and summer, their leaves are a glossy green, but they may also be yellow, red, or a deep maroon. In the fall, poison oak and poison ivy are among the most colorful plants in the woods. To make their identification even more difficult, rare individuals of both species may have not three but *five* leaflets. Both plants drop their leaves during the fall, making them hard to recognize, and it *is* possible to get a rash from touching the naked twigs.

91

Poison Oak
Rhus diversiloba

Kristin Jakob -77

Location: Poison ivy is found throughout the continental United States, except in California, and in Canada and Mexico. Poison oak is found in California, Oregon, Washington, northern Mexico, and southern British Columbia. It is most common in California. In southern Oregon, where both plants are found, poison oak and poison ivy sometimes interbreed, producing seeds that grow into poisonous hybrids.

How They Poison: The sticky sap of both poison oak and poison ivy contains a mixture of chemicals called *catechols*, which cause an allergic skin rash.

The usual way to get a case of poison oak or poison ivy is, of course, to touch the plant, but there are other ways. The poisonous substances in both plants are contained in their oily sap. This sap is very sticky and will cling to clothing, tools, or anything else it touches. If someone later touches one of these objects, he or she may develop a rash. The oils retain their strength for many years: it is possible to develop a rash from touching dead leaves in the middle of the winter or from handling tools that have not been used for many months. Dogs and cats are very common carriers of the poisonous oils. They cannot develop a rash, but they can carry the oil around on their fur and transfer it to any unsuspecting person who pets them.

The very worst cases of poison oak and poison ivy occur when the plants are burned. The toxic oils are carried by the smoke and settle on everything in its path. If the smoke is inhaled, a rash may develop inside the lungs. People who develop poison ivy rash in their lungs are frequently hospitalized, and some have died.

There is no truth to the common belief that one can contract a case of poison ivy by touching the blisters of someone who already has the rash.

Poison Ivy
Rhus radicans

Kristin. Jakob–77

NOTE: Eastern poison oak (*Toxicodendron quericipolium*) is similar to both poison oak and poison ivy but has leaves covered with soft hairs. Eastern poison oak is found along the East Coast from New Jersey to Florida and as far west as Texas and Kansas. It grows on poor, sandy soils.

If you were to ask your friends to name a poisonous plant, they would probably say "poison ivy" unless they came from California, in which case they would say "poison oak." These plants are responsible for the overwhelming majority of all cases of plant poisoning in the United States. Every year more than one million Americans suffer from poison ivy or poison oak rash.

The pictures in this book will help you to recognize the two plants, but the best way to identify them is to observe actual living plants.

The rashes that are produced by poison oak and poison ivy are identical; what is true for one is true for the other. If you suspect that you have been in contact with either plant (most people don't know until it's too late), you can remove much of the poisonous oil by washing immediately with *soap and water*. Washing with water alone will not help because water will only spread the oil. Unfortunately, soap and water are not always available when one is hiking in the country. Still, lathering yourself and washing your hair and your clothing after a trip through poison oak or poison ivy country is always a good idea.

If you have come in contact with the oil, a rash will probably develop within a day or two. Sometimes as much as a week will elapse before the rash develops. If you have a mild rash, you can control the itching with one of many lotions and ointments available at the drugstore without a prescription. The rash will take from a few days to a few weeks to go away. In severe cases, your doctor will probably prescribe a drug called *cortisone* to reduce the swelling.

Hard as it may be, you should never scratch the raw blisters that form because you might develop an infection that could be worse than the rash itself.

Poison oak and poison ivy are members of the Sumac family, a group of about six hundred different species growing throughout the warm and temperate regions of the world. Most members of the family are harmless to man, and, as we shall see, many are very useful plants.

The few sumacs that are harmful produce almost identical effects: they cause itching, swelling, and painful blisters on those parts of the body that have touched the plant. Strictly speaking, these harmful sumacs are not truly "poisonous" plants. Instead, the rashes that they produce are allergic reactions — poison ivy poisoning is an allergy. This is why some people may handle these plants and never suffer the slightest ill effect.

If you are one of the lucky ones who is not allergic to the members of the Sumac family, you may not always be so lucky. Allergies change at different times in a person's life. As you grow older you may gain, lose, and regain an allergy several times. Doctors estimate that more than half of the people in the United States are allergic to poison oak or poison ivy, making this one of the most common allergies known.

Not all of the members of the sumac family have been analyzed chemically, but in those that have the allergy-producing substance appears to be a mixture of chemical compounds called *catechols*, which are found in the oily sap. When touched, the sap is quickly absorbed by the skin — the entire process takes about ten minutes.

96

The Indians, who lived in North America for thousands of years before the first European explorers arrived, were quite familiar with poison oak and poison ivy. Though the Indians sometimes suffered from rashes and itching after touching the plants, this was very rare. They were much less sensitive than the white men.

Poison oak and poison ivy were put to many useful purposes by several American Indian tribes. Some California tribes used poison oak sap and leaves in cures for warts, ringworm, and rattlesnake bite. Others in California mixed the leaves and sap with acorn meal to make bread. Obviously poison oak rash was not a problem in those tribes. The sap of poison oak turns a deep black when it is exposed to air. The Pomo Indians of northern California took advantage of this property to make a dye for their baskets. In eastern North America, the Meskwaki and Potawatomi tribes applied poison ivy leaves to certain kinds of swellings.

The first European explorer to mention poison ivy was Captain John Smith, leader of the English colony at Jamestown, Virginia. This is the same Captain Smith, according to legend, whose life was saved by the Indian Princess Pocahontas. Her father, Chief Powhatan, ordered his warriors to kill the English captain with their war clubs, but Pocahontas covered Smith with her body so the warriors could not strike for fear of harming her. Whether or not the legend is true will probably never be known, but it is certainly true that Captain Smith did see poison ivy in Virginia. In 1612 he published a book in which he described a curious plant of the New World that resembled English "Yvie" but "causeth redness, itchynge, and finally blysters."

Poison Sumac

Other Common Name: Poison elder

Scientific name: *Toxicodendron vernix*

Description: A woody shrub or small tree, growing as high as fifteen feet, with narrow, pointed leaflets in groups of seven to thirteen.

Location: East of the Mississippi River; north to Quebec and south to Florida.

How It Poisons: Poison sumac has the reputation of being the most poisonous member of the Sumac family, probably because it grows in swamps and bogs where the thick vegetation and muddy soil make it difficult to walk without touching the plant. The poisonous substances and symptoms are the same as those of poison oak and poison ivy.

Poison Sumac
Rhus vernix

Poisonwood

Other Common Name: None

Scientific Name: *Metopium toxiferum*

Description: A shrub or small tree. Each leaf has five to seven leaflets. The fruit is about one inch long.

Location: In the United States, only in the Florida Everglades. Various species of *Metopium* grow throughout the Caribbean islands.

How It Poisons: The poisonous substances and symptoms are the same as those of poison oak and poison ivy.

Poisonwood
Metopium toxiferum

Mango

Other Common Name: None

Scientific Name: *Mangifera indica*

Description: A large, evergreen fruit tree, sixty feet high or taller. The peach-colored fruit, which is delicious, may weigh several pounds each.

Location: Mangos are cultivated for their fruit throughout the tropical and subtropical regions of the world. In the United States, it is grown in Hawaii and Florida.

How It Poisons: The fruit stalks (*pedicels*) contain the same poisonous substances as those found in poison oak and poison ivy. Even the mangos sold in grocery stores may have a small amount of this allergy-producing sap clinging to their skin, so it is a good idea to peel the skin before eating a mango.

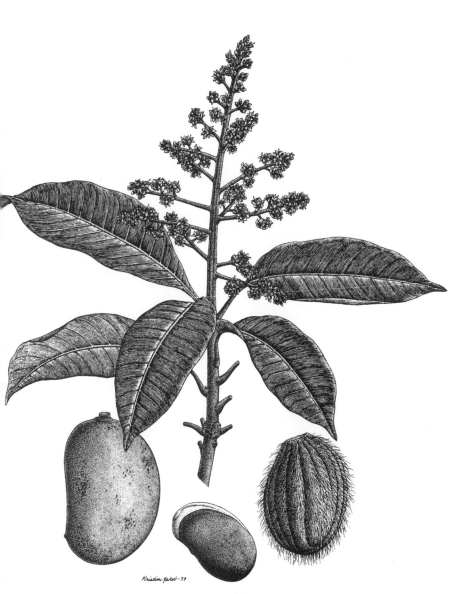

Mango
Mangifera indica

Deadly Hemlock

Other Common Name: Spotted hemlock

Scientific Name: *Conium maculatum*

Description: The hollow stems reach from four to eight feet high. The leaves are lacy and fernlike. Small white flowers grow in umbrella-shaped clusters at the tips of branches. The stem is marked with reddish purple spots, hence its name.

Location: Originally a native of Europe, it grows throughout the world. It is found throughout the continental United States and in Canada. It is very common along the sides of country roads.

How It Poisons: The spotted hemlock contains a mixture of poisonous alkaloids, of which the most important is *coniine*. The stem and leaves are the most poisonous parts of the plant. For a description of the symptoms see the text.

There are three kinds of hemlocks growing in the United States. One is a tall, evergreen tree of the northern forests. The other two are flowering herbs. Why all of these plants are called hemlock is a mystery; in fact, the origin of the word is unknown. But this much is known: the tree is definitely not poisonous, while both of the herbs can be deadly.

Kristin Jakob 77

Hemlock
Conium maculatum

The poisonous hemlocks belong to the parsley family (*Umbelliferae*), which includes such common plants as carrots, celery, and parsnips. Many of the wild plants that are in this family look very much alike: poisonous species are easily confused with edible plants. The leaves of the spotted hemlock (*Conium*) resemble parsley and its seeds look like anise.

The spotted hemlock is perhaps the world's most famous poisonous plant, because almost twenty-four hundred years ago it was used to execute the great philosopher Socrates. His crime, according to the politicians who controlled the city of Athens, was that he had "corrupted the youth of the city" and had "neglected the gods whom the city worships." In truth, Socrates had committed no crime at all. Instead, he had been the friend of other politicians who had fallen from favor and power and who had been the bitter enemies of the men who had then come to power.

There is evidence that the officials of Athens did not really want Socrates to die; he was given many chances to plead guilty and receive a light sentence and even to escape. But Socrates steadfastly refused to admit any guilt or to run away, and so he was put to death. At that time, noble Greeks were killed by being forced to drink a potion made from the leaves of the spotted hemlock. The philosopher Plato has described the death of Socrates in the *Phaedon:*

> When we saw that he was drinking, and actually had drunk the poison, we could no longer restrain our tears . . . I did not weep for his fate, so much as for the loss of a friend and benefactor . . . Socrates, after walking about, now told us that his legs were beginning to grow heavy, and immediately laid down, for so he had been ordered. At the same time the man who had given him the poison examined his feet and legs, touching them at inter-

vals. At length he pressed violently upon his feet, and asked if he felt it. To which Socrates replied that he did not. The man then pressed his legs and so on, showing us that he was becoming cold and stiff. And Socrates, feeling it himself, assured us that when the effects had ascended to his heart, he should then be gone.

The symptoms of spotted hemlock poisoning come on rapidly. Within fifteen minutes to an hour after swallowing enough of the seeds, roots, or leaves, victims may feel nervous and begin to tremble. Later, the hands and feet become numb, just as Socrates' had felt. The heartbeat slows down and the body feels cold. If the victim has eaten a lethal dose, death will come from failure to breathe.

Spotted hemlock is very poisonous to both human beings and animals, but since it has such a bitter taste and unpleasant smell there have been few cases of accidental poisoning. One author has compared the smell of spotted hemlock to that of cat urine.

Water Hemlock

Other Common Names: Cowbane, poison parsnip, snakeroot, spotted hemlock, deadly hemlock, wild carrot, wild parsnip, beaver poison.

Scientific Name: Various species of *Cicuta*

Description: Mature plants stand three to ten feet tall. Their stems are hollow and are often covered with purple spots. During the summer, small white flowers appear in umbrella-shaped clusters. Each leaf is divided into smaller leaflets. The leaves do not have the fernlike appearance of *Conium maculatum*. The roots look very much like parsnips, though they may be covered with smaller rootlets that are shaped something like sweet potatoes. When the stem is cut, droplets of yellow liquid will appear. This liquid smells like a raw parsnip, causing some people to mistake the plant for an edible species.

Location: Only in wet places — in swamps, bogs, marshes, or along stream banks and ditches. Species of *Cicuta* are known to grow in most of the United States and throughout Canada.

How It Poisons: With the possible exception of the deadly amanita mushroom, water hemlock is *the most poisonous plant growing in the United States*. Within thirty minutes of consuming a poisonous dose of water hemlock, victims start to salivate. This is followed rapidly by muscle tremors and violent convulsions. In severe cases the convulsions come almost con-

Cowbane; Water Hemlock
Cicuta virosa

Krishn Jakob-77

tinuously. Death, if it comes, is from failure to breathe. The root is the most poisonous part of the plant, though all parts are dangerous. A single mouthful of the root is enough to kill an adult. Children have been poisoned after sucking on the stems of water hemlock. Not long ago a camper in the Santa Cruz Mountains of northern California died after eating the leaves of western water hemlock (*Cicuta douglasii*), which he thought were watercress leaves. Watercress is a member of the mustard family and looks nothing like water hemlock. The poisonous substance in the water hemlock is called *cicutoxin*. Chemically, it is a form of alcohol.

Oleander

Other Common Name: None

Scientific Name: *Nerium oleander*

Description: An evergreen shrub (sometimes planted in hedges) with large, attractive pink or white flowers and tough, narrow leaves.

Location: Originally a native of the southern European countries, oleander is today grown in warmer climates throughout the world. In the United States, it is found in the southern states and in California and Hawaii.

How It Poisons: Oleander poison acts very much like digitalis, the poison in the foxglove. It causes stomach pain, vomiting, and irregularities in the heartbeat. There may be enough poison in a single oleander leaf to kill an adult, though most cases of accidental poisoning do not end in death. Clippings from oleander plants can be poisonous to horses and cattle. Horses should never be tied to oleander bushes because in just a few minutes the animals can eat enough leaves to become very sick or even die. The bark of the oleander is also poisonous. There is at least one recorded case of a group of people being poisoned at a cookout when they used oleander twigs to roast hot dogs over an open fire. The fire caused the poisonous sap to seep out of the bark and into the meat.

Oleander
Nerium oleander

English Ivy

Other Common Name: None

Scientific Name: *Hedera helix*

Description: English ivy has two quite different growth forms, depending on its age. Young plants grow as climbing vines with three- or five-pointed leaves. More mature plants grow as shrubs with smooth-edged leaves. Only the mature plants produce flowers and fruit (a dark purple berry).

Location: The plant probably got its name from the fact that it is often seen growing along the walls of English homes and gardens, but the plant came originally from Eurasia. Today it is cultivated throughout the world, especially in the temperate climates.

How It Poisons: The symptoms of English ivy poisoning have been described as "excitement" and difficulty in breathing. The quantity of berries needed to cause human poisoning has not been established, but it is probably very large. Nevertheless, children should not be allowed to eat any ivy berries.

English Ivy
Hedera helix

Kristin Jakob 76

St. John's Wort

Other Common Names: Klamath weed, goatweed

Scientific Name: *Hypericum perforatum*

Description: A perennial plant that grows from a woody base. Most plants are one to three feet tall, but may be larger. The small leaves (one-half to one inch long) are attached directly to the stem without a leaf stalk (*petiole*). The leaves are covered with tiny, dark spots that appear translucent when the leaf is held up to a light. The flowers are yellow, have five petals, and measure about an inch across.

Location: A native of Europe, St. John's Wort now grows in most of the United States and Canada. Many closely related species (some also poisonous) are found in North America.

How It Poisons: St. John's Wort is a *photosensitizer* (see below).

When the European settlers came to the New World they brought along the seeds of many different plants. Some seeds were brought intentionally, to start the crops that the settlers had grown back in the Old World. Other seeds made the trip by accident, either mixed in with the crop seeds or clinging to a piece of clothing — or perhaps stuck to the hair of the goats, pigs, and cattle that the settlers brought for their farms. Perhaps

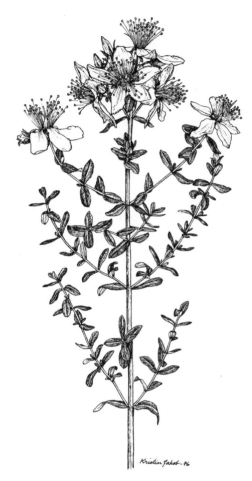

St. John's Wort
Hypericum perforatum

one tenth of all the different kinds of plants growing in the United States came from the Old World originally.

One of the seeds that came accidentally grew into a shrubby, yellow-flowered herb called St. John's Wort, or Klamath weed. No one knows for sure when St. John's Wort first appeared in America, but by 1900 the plant was growing throughout the United States and Canada. At about that time it was brought into California from neighboring states. As so often happens when a new plant is brought into California's mild climate, this one ran wild. By 1951 St. John's Wort was growing in 2,333,000 acres of California fields and pastures and was crowding out other plants. The spread of St. John's Wort caused the California ranchers much concern because they knew that it was poisoning their livestock by the thousands, causing them to lose millions of dollars.

Animals that eat St. John's Wort develop symptoms that are the same as those of a very bad sunburn. The parts of their skin not covered with hair become red, swollen, and itchy. In severe cases, pieces of skin die and peel off the animal, leaving bleeding sores. Yet this "sunburn" is rarely severe enough to kill the animal by itself. Most deaths are caused by starvation because the animals' mouths become so badly burned that they are unable to eat.

Farm animals do not normally develop sunburn. Most of their bodies are covered with hair, and the exposed parts — their ears, eyes, udders, and mouths — contain pigments that protect the skin against light. But some poisonous substances can cause animals to develop a great sensitivity to light, a condition that veterinarians call *photosensitivity*. The chemicals that cause photosensitivity are called *photosensitizers*. St. John's Wort contains a powerful photosensitizer, a chemical called *hypericin*. Several other plants, including bluegreen algae, wild buckwheats, and some kinds of clover, also produce photosensitizers.

In 1946, agricultural scientists began an experiment to see if St. John's Wort could be eliminated from pasturelands by a small insect with the not-so-small name of *Chrysolina quadrigemina*. *C. quadrigemina* (for short) is an Australian beetle with a very specific diet: it eats St. John's Wort and a few related species, but it does not harm other plants. In 1951 large numbers of these beetles were released into the California fields and their effect was impressive. In less than ten years 99 per cent of the St. John's Wort in California had been removed. More important, the number of animals poisoned by the plant dropped sharply. Today, St. John's Wort is only a minor problem for farmers in the United States and Canada.

The success of this effort to control St. John's Wort is strong proof that we do not always have to use herbicides and other strong chemicals to remove undesirable plants. Biological control — using one natural process to control another — is often the best way to eliminate a pest without damaging the environment.

Christmas Rose

Other Common Name: Black hellebore

Scientific Name: *Helleborus niger*

Description: A perennial herb that stands about one foot high, it is not a rose at all, but rather a member of the buttercup family. The plant takes the name "rose" because it has large, attractive flowers. It is called a Christmas rose because, in warm climates, it flowers during the winter, often at Christmastime. The underground portion of the stem and the roots are black, hence the name black hellebore.

Location: A native of Europe, today grown in flower gardens throughout the United States.

How It Poisons: Christmas rose contains at least three different poisons. One of these poisons, *helleborein*, is in the juice of the plant. If the plant is bruised, the juice may seep out and cause a skin rash if it is touched. The plant is much more dangerous if eaten because it contains poisons that act on the heart and on the nervous system. Christmas rose poisoning is rare and usually not fatal, but it can make a person very sick.

In the past, extract of Christmas rose was sometimes prescribed as a laxative, but this treatment surely must have poisoned as

Christmas Rose or Hellebore
Helleborus niger

Kristin Jakob '77

many patients as it cured. An English medical book published nearly a hundred and fifty years ago had this to say about the Christmas rose: "Were it expunged [removed] from our materia medica [list of medicines], we could easily fill up the vacancy by . . . plants of greater value." Indeed, that vacancy has been filled. Today the Christmas rose is grown only for its beautiful flowers.

Monkshood

Other Common Names: Aconite, wolfbane, friar's cap

Scientific Name: *Aconitum napellus* (and other closely related species of *Aconitum*)

Description: A perennial herb standing about three feet tall, it has many leaves that, in outline, resemble a bird's footprints. The flowers are a deep blue-violet. It takes its name from the fact that the uppermost petal of each flower is shaped very much like the hood of a monk's cloak.

Location: *Aconitum napellus* is a native of Europe and Asia. Today it is cultivated in flower gardens throughout the United States for use in homeopathic medicine "(treatment of disease by giving small doses of drugs that, in large doses, cause symptoms like those of the disease)". Other species of *Aconitum*, both wild and cultivated, are found in the United States.

How It Poisons: The roots and seeds are the most dangerous parts of the plant, but the leaves are also poisonous. All parts of the plant contain the poisonous substance *aconitine*. Aconitine poisons the vagus nerve, which connects the brain with the heart. If a lethal dose of monkshood has been consumed, death from heart failure may come within two hours.

Monkshood
Aconitum napellus

Kristin Jakob . 76

Monkshood is a deadly poisonous plant. In earlier times monkshood was used to make arrow poisons, and the "master poisoners" of the sixteenth century often included extract of monkshood in their "tool kits." Extract of monkshood, which is also known as *aconite*, has sometimes been used as a medicine, but its dangers far outweigh its advantages. There are several known cases of human poisoning from using the leaves of monkshood to make a salad. Horses, cattle, sheep, and goats have died after grazing on the flowers, leaves, and roots of wild species of *Aconitum*. A far greater threat to cattle, however, is the wild larkspurs (*Delphinium*). Larkspur is a close relative of monkshood (both are members of the Buttercup family), and the blue- or purple-flowered larkspurs look very much like monkshood.

The other common name for monkshood, wolfbane, means "wolf poison." There is a legend that the flowers and leaves of the wolfbane are a charm that will protect people against werewolves!

The Nightshades:

Belladonna, Henbane, Jimsonweed

Less than eighty years ago, the great American horticulturist George Washington Carver did something that some people thought was very dangerous: he ate a tomato! There was, of course, nothing dangerous about what Carver was doing — the tomato was tasty and full of vitamins and minerals. In fact, Caver ate the tomato in order to convince other people that they should include this safe and nutritious food in their diet. Yet it is not too surprising that some people feared the plant, because the tomato is a member of the Nightshade family, which has long had a reputation of being poisonous.

The tomato is not the only nonpoisonous nightshade. Peppers, potatoes, and eggplants are also members of the Nightshade family. Tobacco too is a nightshade, and although many people do not consider it poisonous, it most certainly is. Cattle will die if they eat too much tobacco, and there is a great deal of evidence that people who smoke tobacco are harming their health.

But the plants that have given the Nightshade family most of its sinister reputation are the mandrake, henbane, belladonna, and various members of the genus *Datura*. In the United States, the most widely distributed species of *Datura* is *D. stramonium*, better known as jimsonweed, or thornapple.

The very name "nightshade" conjures up visions of evil — of

witchcraft, sorcery, and death. This is no accident, for these plants have been a favorite ingredient in witches' brews and murderers' potions for thousands of years.

All of these plants are poisonous because they contain two chemical substances, *atropine* and *scopolamine*, which interfere with the nervous system. The symptoms normally seen include an unusually fast heartbeat, a dry mouth, dilated pupils, flushed skin, fever, and a general relaxation of the smooth muscles. Death is rare in cases of accidental nightshade poisoning, but when it does occur it is usually the result of either heart failure or failure to breathe. The symptoms of nightshade poisoning have been described in a medical textbook as "hot as a hare, blind as a bat, dry as a bone, red as a beet, and mad [crazy] as a wet hen." In very young children, atropine poisoning may produce a dangerously high fever (109° F; 42.8° C), and the victims must be treated with ice packs and sponge baths to cool them off. Poisoning victims are kept in darkened rooms because their pupils are so greatly dilated (expanded) that even normal amounts of light can harm the eyes.

Most cases of atropine and scopolamine poisoning seen by doctors are not caused by accidentally eating the plants; they are caused by an overdose of medicine that contains an extract of the plant. A modern medical textbook states: "It is a rare home that does not have at least one preparation containing atropine or some other belladonna extract in the medicine cabinet." Contac cold medicine, Sominex sleeping pills, and Asthmador asthma powder are just a few of these medicines. All of these medications are dangerous if taken in excess.

Extracts of the poisonous nightshades have been used as medicines for at least three thousand years. The scientific name of the Nightshade family, *Solanaceae*, comes from the Latin word *solamen*, which means "quieting." This refers to the fact that the poisonous nightshades have long been used as sedatives. In earlier days, the dried leaves of the deadly nightshade were crushed and smoked as a remedy for asthma. Today, extracts of the nightshades, or synthetic drugs that closely resemble them, are used to stimulate the heart, control muscle spasms, control colic, and cure ulcers. Atropine is still used by eye doctors to dilate the pupils and is also used as an antidote in certain kinds of insecticide poisoning.

The long association of the nightshades with witchcraft and black magic is undoubtedly due to the powerful effects that atropine and scopolamine have on the mind. In sufficient amounts, the drugs will cause hallucinations and symptoms of madness. For a time it was believed that scopolamine might be used as a truth serum — that a person taking the drug would not be able to lie or keep a secret — but this is not true.

There are many legends that tell of witches flying through the air. In some, the witches fly astride enchanted animals or on the back of Satan himself; in others, the witches fly on a stick. The witch on a broomstick is a popular image in European and American folklore. Many of the old texts on witchcraft tell of how witches first had to anoint themselves with a special "flying ointment" and recite magical chants before they could fly. Almost all of the recipes for flying ointment included one or more of the poisonous nightshades. A recipe that was used by English witches during the sixteenth century called for a mixture of soot, henbane, deadly nightshade, and the fat from a stillborn baby.

Whether or not witches can fly is really not a question for science, but it is certainly true that if witches rubbed themselves with such an ointment they may have *thought* they were flying.

Atropine and scopolamine can penetrate the skin and, in sufficient amounts, cause hallucinations. If the witches believed that the ointment would help them fly, their hallucinations may have included visions of flight.

Belladonna

Other Common Names: Deadly nightshade, poison cherry

Scientific Name: *Atropa belladonna*

Description: An herb that grows to a height of two to five feet. The stem is covered with short hairs and the root is thick and fleshy with several branches. The leaves are about six inches long with smooth margins. The flowers are about an inch long, have five petals that are a dull purple at their tip and yellowish at their base. The fruit is a dark purple (almost black) and about the size of a small cherry.

Location: A native of southern Europe and the Middle East. During the First and Second World Wars, the plant was cultivated in the United States and used in the manufacture of medicines because it was difficult to import enough of it. Very little deadly nightshade is grown commercially in the United States today, but this attractive plant is grown in flower gardens in many parts of the country and is occasionally seen growing wild.

How It Poisons: See page 132.

According to ancient Greek legend, the deadly nightshade was first cultivated by the sorceress/goddess Hecate, who kept the

Deadly Nightshade
Atropa bella-donna

Kristin Jakob . 76

plant in a garden surrounded by high walls and guarded by fierce demons. Other legends tell how the Devil himself kept a garden of deadly nightshade that he tended every night except Walpurgis Night (April 30), when he presided at the witches' Sabbath.

The scientific name of the species, *belladonna*, is an Italian word meaning "beautiful woman" and comes from the fact that Italian women of the fifteenth and sixteenth centuries used the juice of the plant as a beauty aid. Large eyes were considered beautiful, so the women would place a drop of the juice in their eyes to dilate their pupils.

More than two thousand years ago, the Roman historian Plutarch reported an epidemic of nightshade poisoning among Marc Antony's troops. Marc Antony's army was camped far from home and the soldiers were not familiar with the local plants. As Plutarch tells it:

> Those who sought for herbs and pot-herbs obtained few that they had been accustomed to eat, and in tasting unknown herbs, they found one that brought on madness and death. He that had eaten it immediately lost all memory and knowledge; but at the same time would busy himself in turning and moving every stone he met with as if he was upon some very important pursuit. The camp was full of unhappy men, bending to the ground; and thus digging up and removing stones . . .

NOTE: In the United States, most cases of human poisoning attributed to deadly nightshade are caused, not by belladonna, but by two other plants know as *bittersweets*. Both of these plants contain poisonous alkaloids that produce symptoms resembling belladonna poisoning. Both plants are members of the Nightshade family, belonging to the genus *Solanum* (the same genus as the potato!). A description of these plants follows:

European Bittersweet

Other Common Names: Woody nightshade, blue nightshade, climbing nightshade, deadly nightshade

Scientific Name: *Solanum dulcamara*

Description: A woody plant that sometimes climbs like a vine. Large plants may be six feet long. The leaves are pointed and have smooth margins. The flowers are white, purplish white, or deep blue. The fruit is a bright red berry.

Location: Originally a native of Europe, the plant now grows wild in woods throughout North America.

How It Poisons: The symptoms of European bittersweet poisoning are similar to those of belladonna poisoning. The victims are usually young children who mistake the berries for cherries.

Kristin Jakob -77

European Bittersweet
Solanum dulcamora

American Bittersweet

Other Common Names: Black nightshade, deadly nightshade, poison berry

Scientific Name: *Solanum nigrum*

Description: The leaves and flowers are similar to those of the European bittersweet. The American bittersweet is a smaller plant with a green (not woody) stem and dark purple or black berries.

Location: American bittersweet is most common in the eastern United States.

How They Poison: See the description of belladonna poisoning on page 132.

Black Henbane

Other Common Names: Stinking nightshade, fetid nightshade, stinking roger

Scientific Name: *Hyoscyamus niger*

Description: A stout herb about two feet tall with toothed leaves from three to eight inches long. The entire plant is covered with soft hairs and is somewhat "clammy" to the touch. The flowers are an inch or two in diameter with yellow petals and purple veins. The fruit is green, less than an inch in diameter, and enclosed within the calyx.

Location: Henbane is a native of the Old World and, like belladonna, was cultivated in the United States during the two world wars as a source of medicine. Some henbane has escaped from cultivation and grows wild in the nothern United States and southern Canada. It is most common in some of the Rocky Mountain States.

How It Poisons: See the description of belladonna poisoning on page 132.

Henbane is an Old English word meaning "hen poison." Apparently the plant got its name from the observation that chickens will die from eating henbane seed.

Henbane

Hyoseyamus niger

Jimsonweed

Other Common Name: Thornapple, stinkweed

Scientific Name: *Datura stramonium*

Description: Jimsonweed grows from three to five feet tall. Like henbane, jimsonweed has a very unpleasant smell; in some parts of the country its common name is "stinkweed." Perhaps its most distinctive features are its large flowers and spiny fruits. The flower is white (sometimes a pale violet) and about four inches long. The fruit is green, about two inches long, and covered with large spines.

Location: Jimsonweed is a native American nightshade that probably originated in the tropical regions of Central and South America and that now grows throughout the continental United States, Canada, and Hawaii. The plant takes its common name from Jamestown, Virginia, where, in 1676, a group of English soldiers were poisoned after they used the leaves of the plant in a salad.

How It Poisons: The whole plant is poisonous, and even the nectar from the flower contains enough poison to make a child sick. When the plant is young, before the flowers or fruit have appeared, it is still very poisonous. Symptoms of jimsonweed poisoning are similar to those of belladonna poisoning. Victims of jimsonweed poisoning tend to be older than the victims of most other poisonous plants. Typically these victims are teen-

Jimsonweed
Datura stramonium

Kristin Jakob-77

agers or young adults who deliberately eat the plant for its psychedelic effects and poison themselves in the process. Overdoses of jimsonweed can be fatal.

There are several other species of *Datura* that grow in the United States, and some are also cultivated for their attractive flowers. The most common is *D. meteloides*, which grows in California, Colorado, and throughout the southwestern states. *D. meteloides* has large white flowers from six to eight inches long. The plant is quite attractive. Among several Indian tribes of California and the Southwest, the plant was used in the ceremonies that marked a boy's passage to manhood. The boys were first given a tea brewed from the plant and then required to join in a ceremonial dance. Then the boys would drift off into a drugged sleep. When they awoke there would be much discussion of the meaning of their dreams and the significance they might have for each boy's new life as a man.

Castor Bean

Other Common Names: Castor oil plant, palma Christi

Scientific Name: *Ricinus communis*

Description and Location: Depending on the climate in which it is grown, the castor bean can be anything from a small shrub to a large tree. In warm climates, such as the southern United States and California, the plant forms a small tree. In tropical Asia and Africa it often grows to heights of forty feet. In more temperate climates, the northern United States, for example, the plant seldom grows much taller than five or six feet and will not survive the winter. No matter what its size, if the plant produces fruit it is potentially dangerous because each fruit contains three poisonous seeds.

The seeds of castor bean are very distinctive: each is about three quarters of an inch long and is a glossy brown, as though it has been painted with a shiny lacquer. On the surface of each seed is a pattern of thin white, brown, or black lines. The seed looks very much like a fat, blood-filled tick. In fact, the scientific name of the genus, *Ricinus*, is also the scientific name of a tick (the Mediterranean sheep tick, to be exact). The plant was given this name because of the resemblance of its seeds to the animal.

How It Poisons: The seeds contain a strong poison called *ricine* — as few as two seeds can be fatal if chewed and swallowed. In its mildest form, ricine poisoning produces a burning

Kristin Jakob - 76

Castor Oil Plant
Ricinus communis

sensation in the mouth; in severe cases it produces violent convulsions and death from failure to breathe. Young children are especially susceptible to castor bean poisoning because they will use the shiny seeds as toys and put them in their mouths. In warmer parts of the United States, castor bean is often planted in gardens because it grows very fast. Within a few years the plants may reach a height of ten feet or more. A single plant of this size may drop thousands of seeds onto the ground and into the reach of small children.

Castor bean is also a useful plant. Castor oil, which is squeezed from the seeds, is used both as a laxative and in the manufacture of several products, including cosmetics, printer's ink, and machine oil. Most of the world's castor oil is produced in Africa and India, but some is also produced in the United States. Castor oil is not poisonous, but the remains of the seeds after the oil has been squeezed from them are still dangerous. These squashed seeds, which are known as "press cake," have been accidentally fed to farm animals with disastrous results.

Foxglove

Other Common Name: None

Scientific Name: *Digitalis purpurea*

Description: Mature foxglove plants may stand six or more feet high with large clusters of leaves at their base and a dense cluster of purple or white flowers at their tip. The flowers are bell-shaped, somewhat resembling the fingers of a glove.

Location: A native of Europe, it is now cultivated in flower gardens throughout the world. The plant often escapes from cultivation and grows wild along the West Coast of the United States.

How It Poisons: See below.

Heart disease is a terrible problem in the United States. More than one million Americans suffer from some kind of heart disease, and the number keeps going up year by year. Why this is so is not completely understood, but several factors seem to contribute to the increase in heart disease, including cigarette smoking, eating too many fatty foods, being overweight, and having high blood pressure. Each year, more than 700,000 people die from heart disease. Many of those who have heart disease depend for their survival on a drug called *digitalis*. Digi-

Foxglove
Digitalis purpurea

talis comes from a poisonous plant, the beautiful garden flower that we call the foxglove.

In about half of all cases of heart disease, patients develop *congestive heart failure.* This condition develops when the heart becomes so weak that it is unable to pump blood through the body fast enough. As a result, blood and other fluids begin to collect in the lungs and in other parts of the body. Breathing becomes very difficult and the skin may become swollen. If these fluids are not removed quickly, the heart may stop beating altogether and the patient will die. For about two hundred years, digitalis from the foxglove has been the best medicine for controlling congestive heart failure. Even the best chemical laboratories have so far failed to synthesize a better drug.

Digitalis has two major effects on the body. First, it strengthens the heartbeat, causing the circulation of blood to speed up. Second, it helps the body eliminate the fluids that are clogging up the lungs and blood vessels.

Digitalis is truly a "wonder drug," but it is also a *dangerous* drug that has poisoned many people. Most drugs have what is called a *factor of safety* — the difference between the amount of a drug that is good for the patient and the amount that may be dangerous. The factor of safety for digitalis is very low, less than twice the normal dose will often produce dangerous symptoms. Overdoses can make the heart speed up, skip beats, or, even worse, stop altogether. When doctors prescribe digitalis they regulate the amount carefully.

As the number of people suffering from heart disease has increased, so has the number of cases of accidental digitalis poisoning. Most of these poisoning victims are older people who have taken an accidental overdose. But the number of young children who are poisoned by digitalis is also increasing. Almost all of these have been poisoned by digitalis that was carelessly left lying about the house. Digitalis has a faintly sweet taste (the drug is chemically related to sugar) that a child might mistake for candy. Children have also been accidentally poisoned by nibbling on the leaves and flowers of the foxglove plant, but this happens rarely since the plant does not taste good at all.

Many of the poisonous plants that furnish medicines have been known for thousands of years, but the properties of foxglove were discovered rather recently. Foxglove was first mentioned as a medicine in 1542 by a German herbalist, Leonhard Fuchs (the beautiful garden flower called the fuchsia is named after Fuchs). After Fuchs, many different writers began to claim medicinal properties for the foxglove. It was prescribed for epilepsy, diarrhea, gonorrhea, and other diseases (no doubt with many fatal results).

The discovery that foxglove could be useful in treating heart disease is generally credited to William Withering, an English physician of the eighteenth century. Withering learned that a farm family living near his home in Shropshire had had remarkable success in treating the victims of "dropsy," the name given to a disease caused by an abnormal accumulation of fluids in the body, which caused its victims to become quite swollen. Today we know that most cases of dropsy are actually the result of congestive heart failure.

Withering investigated the farmers' cure and found that they were using a blend of herbs that included the leaves of the foxglove plant. Soon Withering began using floxglove to treat dropsy patients. He was so impressed with the success of this new medicine that in 1785 he published a book describing it to his fellow physicians. It was Withering who first showed that digitalis had its main effect on the heart.

In Withering's time, it was customary for dropsy patients to take digitalis either by eating the dried and powdered leaves or by drinking a solution made by soaking the leaves in water or alcohol. Although the leaves are still used as a medicine, today most digitalis medicines are made from the pure chemical *digitoxin*, which also comes from the foxglove plant. The advantage of using pure digitoxin is that it allows doctors to be more certain of the exact amount of the drug that they are giving their patients.

FLOWERING PLANTS (TREES)

Manchineel

Other Common Name: None

Scientific Name: *Hippomane mancinella*

Description: Manchineel is an attractive tree, standing ten to twenty feet tall. Very old manchineel trees may reach a height of forty feet. The leaves are two to four inches long with a deep, glossy green color. The fruits look like small yellow apples an inch or two in diameter and are sometimes streaked with red.

Location: The manchineel grows along the shores of all the islands in the Caribbean and along the eastern shore of Central America. It is also found in one part of the United States: the extreme southern tip of Florida.

How It Poisons: Manchineel is a member of the Spurge family, a large group of plants that includes the cassava (tapioca), the castor bean, the tung tree, and the poinsettia. Like many spurges, the manchineel produces a thick, milky sap. This sap contains the still-unknown chemical that causes the burning

Manchineel
Hippomane manchinella

and blistering symptoms of manchineel poisoning. The fruits are the most poisonous parts of the plant, containing the poisonous alkaloid *physostigmine*. Eating the fruit may cause severe stomach pain, internal bleeding, and, rarely, death.

On November 3, 1493, on his second voyage to the New World, Christopher Columbus anchored his ship the *Santa Maria* off a small island in the southern Caribbean. Columbus stayed at this island for only one day, for he was anxious to sail north to the island of Hispaniola, where some crew members from the famous first voyage of 1492 had chosen to stay and try to establish a Spanish colony. In his haste, Columbus had barely enough time to row ashore, claim the island for the king and queen of Spain, and give it the name Marie Galante. But the single day was enough for Columbus and his crew to discover that a poisonous tree grew along the shores of the island.

The sailors called the tree *manzanillo*, the Spanish word for "little apple," because its branches were covered with small, sweet-smelling fruit that looked very much like little yellow apples. But the *manzanillo*, they soon discovered, was nothing like a real apple tree: when they touched its bark or rubbed against its leaves, the seamen broke out in painful blisters caused by a caustic sap. Fortunately, none of Columbus's men ate the fruit; if they had, they would certainly have become very sick and perhaps have even died.

Other explorers were not so lucky. In the years following Columbus's voyages, many ships sailed the Caribbean and many a poor sailor became sick or died from eating the poisonous "little apple." The *manzanillo*, or manchineel, as it is called in English, proved especially dangerous to shipwrecked sailors who, in their search for food, were sometimes deceived by the inviting odor of the fruit.

Columbus did not actually discover the manchineel. The original inhabitants of the Caribbean islands, the Carib Indians, had long known of the poisonous tree. They blended its sap into several of their medicines and used an extract of its fruit as an arrow poison. When Columbus finally reached the colony at Hispaniola, he found that all of the Spanish colonists had been killed by the Caribs. Perhaps some of these unfortunate Spaniards had been slain with manchineel-poisoned arrows.

The early settlers of Florida and the Caribbean islands removed the manchineel trees that they found growing near their settlements. Chopping down a manchineel was a risky business, for when an ax bit into the tree, the poisonous sap would squirt in all directions. If the sap landed in the wodcutter's eyes, it caused temporary, and sometimes permanent, blindness. Burning down the tree was equally hazardous, because the poisonous sap would be carried by the smoke and everyone who was touched by it could be poisoned.

There is a common belief among many of the people of the Caribbean that a person can be poisoned simply by standing in the shade of a manchineel tree. This is, of course, not true. The belief was probably devised by parents who wanted to scare their children away from the poisonous tree. When these children grew up, they repeated the story to their own children. Within a few generations, no one could remember how the belief had started and it became accepted as truth. But though its shade is not poisonous, the manchineel's leaves, bark, and fruit certainly are. Should you ever travel to the Caribbean or southern Florida and see this tree, you would do well to observe it from a distance.

152

6

Poisonous Plants Around the World

Curare poison

(*Chondodendron tomentosum* and *Strychnos toxifera*)

This book began with the story of curare, with the Indian hunter moving quietly through the jungle with his blowgun and poisoned darts. Such scenes are rare today, perhaps even non-existent. Most Indian hunters in South America now prefer to do their hunting with rifles and bullets. As the dense green jungles of the Amazon and Orinoco rivers are cleared to make way for cattle ranches and highways, the native Indians are being forced either to give up their cultures and accept the white people's ways or to move deeper into the jungle.

Many of the jungle-dwelling Indians have died from diseases that we do not usually think of as being fatal, such as measles or chickenpox. They die from these diseases because they have never before experienced them, and so they have no natural resistance. With each person who dies, the world loses a piece of special knowledge of the jungle plants and how they may be used. In 1960, three years after the first satellite was fired into space, the last curare maker of the Macusi tribe died at his home in British Guiana, taking to his grave the tribe's secret recipe for the arrow poison called *curare*.

Curare has fascinated explorers of the New World since the time of Columbus's voyages. The first stories that came back to Europe told how the Indians had tried to drive off the Spanish soldiers with poisoned arrows. In his book *De Orbe Novo* (The New World), published in 1555, the Italian writer Peter d'Anglera described a battle between the Indians and the Spaniards in which more than thirty Spanish soldiers were killed. "The poison is of such force," he wrote, "that albeit the wounds were not great, yet they died thereof immediately."

The Spanish soldiers were very interested in finding out more about this poison so that they might discover an antidote. One of the first secrets that the Spaniards tried to learn was just what plants went into curare. The Indians, of course, were not anxious to share their secret, since they had every reason to believe that the Spaniards were not their friends. The problem of learning what ingredients were used was made more complicated by the fact that in most tribes the technique for manufacturing curare was a secret entrusted only to certain members, the medicine men. For a time it was believed that sugar or salt could be used as an antidote to curare, but this proved to be completely false. In fact, to this very day no good antidote is known.

D'Anglera's book stated that the arrow poison was made from the poisoned apples of a tree that grew beside the ocean. These apples were said to be the very same fruit that Adam and Eve had eaten before they were driven out of the Garden of Eden. It is very likely that the "apples" mentioned by d'Anglera were actually the fruits of the poisonous manchineel tree, which does grow beside the sea but is not one of the ingredients in curare. Then again, the apples may have been the fruit of a vine that is used in the manufacture of curare. This vine, however, grows deep in the jungle, not by the sea.

The first European explorer to mention curare by name was Lawrence Keymis, an English soldier who went to South America with Sir Walter Raleigh. In 1596 Keymis wrote about a poisonous herb that he called "ourari." Later, other European writers mentioned the poison by several rather similar names such as "wourali," "woorara," "uruara," and "curara." All of these names were really just attempts to write the Indian name for the plant in English. To this day, no one knows what the Indian word for curare really means. Some language experts have suggested that it means "bird kill," while others believe it means "come-fall," as in "whoever it *comes* to *falls* dead."

Major breakthroughs in solving the mystery of curare came in the eighteenth and nineteenth centuries. In 1745 a French scientist, Charles-Marie de la Condamine, obtained a small bit of curare from Indians in the jungles of what is today Ecuador. Condamine sent samples of the poison back to Europe, where other scientists began experimenting with it. Later, two scientists, one English and the other German, were able to collect other Indian recipes for curare and, further, to observe how the poison was brewed. In 1761 the Englishman Edward Bancroft described the curare of the Accawau Indians, which was made from five different plants. The German Alexander von Humboldt observed the preparation of curare by members of a tribe living in what is today Venezuela.

Bancroft's and Humboldt's observations helped establish the fact that many of the important ingredients in curare came from a group of jungle vines. To make curare, the Indian medicine men would boil the bark of the vines in water. Then the bark was removed and the remaining liquid was boiled further. Other plants were then added to the mixture. Some of these other plants made the mixture sticky so it would cling to the point of an arrow. Others were added because they were believed to have magical powers. When the curare-maker finished his job, he was left with a black, sticky mass that looked very much like tar.

The sticky lump of curare could be stored for several years

Strychnos toxifera

without losing its strength. When the hunter needed a fresh supply of poisoned arrows, he would soften the lump of curare by wetting it or holding it in a fire and then dip the tip of an arrow into the poison.

One of the most impressive uses of curare was in the weapon called the blowpipe, or blowgun. The blowgun of the Macusi tribe was a hollow bamboo tube about ten feet long, lined with a hollow reed. The darts used in the blowgun were slivers of palm wood, needle-sharp at one end and blunt at the other. The sharp end of the dart was dipped in curare while the blunt end was wrapped in cotton so it would fit snugly in the blowgun. The Indian hunters shot the darts by blowing through the tube. Blowgun darts could travel as far as three hundred feet. In the hands of a skilled hunter, the blowgun was deadly accurate.

While explorers of South America were learning more about the ingredients of curare, scientists in Europe were trying to find out just how the poison worked. It was soon established that curare did something to make its victim's muscles fail to move, and death from curare came when the muscles used in breathing became paralyzed. In one experiment, performed in 1814, a donkey was given a seemingly fatal dose of curare. But after the poor animal fell to the ground, air was pumped down its windpipe with a bellows. The pumping continued for four hours, after which the donkey stood up, apparently cured. The animal lived for twenty-five more years.

During the hundred and twenty-five years after the experiment with the donkey, scientists made several important discoveries about curare. Botanists helped to establish that the plants the Indians used to make curare were two jungle vines called *Strychnos toxifera* and *Chondodendron tomentosum*, and during the twentieth century chemists were able to extract the actual

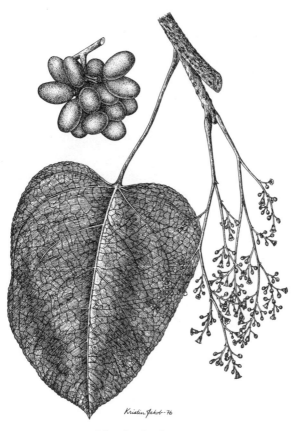

Chondrodendron tomentosum

poisonous chemicals from these vines. Through further experiments, it was discovered that curare poisons act on the exact spot where nerves and muscles join. Normally, the nerves that connect with muscles produce a chemical called *acetylcholine* (a-see-till-*ko*-leen). This chemical passes from the nerve to the muscle and makes it contract. Curare blocks acetylcholine, making it impossible for the muscles to contract. Instead, they relax completely.

Even before they completely understood how curare worked, doctors took advantage of its powers to relax muscles. There are several diseases that have as symptoms a tightening of the muscles. Tetanus, or "lockjaw," is one such disease that is sometimes treated with curare. It is also used in some kinds of surgery to relax the patient's muscles so it is easier for the surgeon's knife to make an incision. But wherever curare is used in medicine, it is always used with great caution because it is still a dangerous poison — every bit as dangerous as the poisonous darts that once came from the hunter's blowgun.

Nutmeg
(*Myristica fragrans*)

In 1512 Dutch traders brought back to Europe a new spice that they had discovered on a small island in the Moluccan Archipelago, a chain of islands that are better known as the Spice Islands. The new spice was called *nutmeg*, and it soon enjoyed great popularity in Europe. Doctors prescribed nutmeg for several different illnesses, and many people believed that nutmegs could be used to brew excellent love potions. They were sometimes covered with silver and worn as charms on chains around the neck. Nutmeg was so popular in Europe that during the eighteenth century there were times when the Dutch imported more than 250,000 pounds of it each year. Most of this nutmeg came from Banda Island, a small piece of land only eight miles long and five miles across. There was so much money to be made selling nutmeg and other spices in Europe that the Dutch, the Portuguese, and the British fought a series of wars for the control of Banda and the other Spice Islands. In 1796 the British took over Banda and began exporting nutmeg trees to plantations in other parts of the world. From Banda Island, nutmegs went to Sumatra, Trinidad, and other tropical islands.

One reason for the nutmeg's popularity, quite aside from its value as a spice, was that the seed had intoxicating properties. Chewing nutmeg seeds brought on feelings of happiness, hallucinations, and a pleasant drowsiness. Yet, as with so many other intoxicating plants, too much nutmeg can be very dangerous. Overdoses of nutmeg produce stomach pains, an abnor-

Nutmeg
Myristica fragrans

mally fast heartbeat, and, in extreme cases, damage to the liver. According to a recent medical book, as few as two whole nutmeg seeds can be fatal!

Nutmeg is the seed of a yellow-flowered tree that grows to a mature height of about thirty feet. This tree produces fruit that looks something like an apricot. Inside each fruit is a seed about one inch long, covered with a bright red tissue called the *aril*. The aril is used to produce a spice called *mace*. Both nutmeg and mace are sold either as whole seeds or as a powder. Just like medicines, both of these spices should be kept out of the reach of young children.

Cashew Nut

(*Anacardium occidentale*)

The delicious cashew nut comes from another poisonous sumac, the evergreen cashew tree, a native of Brazil. Symptoms of cashew poisoning are the same as poison oak or poison ivy rash. The nuts that you purchase are not themselves poisonous; the poisons are contained in the shells, which have long since been discarded. A liquid extracted from the shells of cashew nuts has sometimes been used in manufacturing the insulation for electrical wires used in airplanes. Electricians working on this wiring have sometimes developed painful rashes.

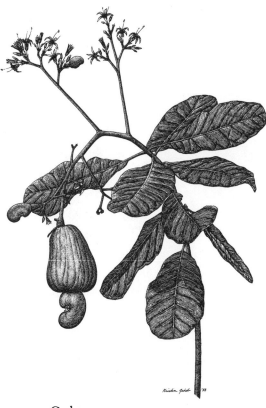

Cashew
Anacardium occidentale

The Lacquer Tree

(*Rhus verniciflua*)

For thousands of years, craftsmen in China and Japan have gathered the sap of another poisonous sumac, the lacquer tree. The sap is used to make a hard, brilliant lacquer that is used to finish wooden bowls, trays, furniture, and musical instruments. Hundreds of years ago, some Chinese noblemen had their entire houses painted with this lacquer.

This lacquer is extremely tough and long-lasting. Not long ago, archaeologists in China opened a tomb that was more than twenty-two hundred years old. Inside the tomb they found many pieces of lacquerware that, when cleaned, were as good as new.

The sap of the lacquer tree is gathered in much the same fashion as maple syrup. The lacquer gatherers make a series of cuts around the base of the tree and on all branches more than an inch in diameter. As the sap oozes from the tree it is collected in small buckets. This process kills the portion of the tree that grows above the ground, but the roots remain alive and, in time, a new shoot grows from them.

When the sap of the lacquer tree is exposed to the air, it turns black and becomes thick and gummy. Before the gummy mixture becomes too thick, it is strained through a cloth to remove any pieces of dirt or bark that may have fallen in. Next, the sap is heated and stirred to a smooth consistency and then stored in airtight vessels so it will not dry out.

It takes twenty to thirty coats of lacquer and at least eighteen

Rhus verniciflua

days to produce a finished piece of lacquerware. Each coat must dry for twelve to twenty-four hours. Artisans will sometimes mix charcoal, lampblack, lead, and even gold and silver with the lacquer to create special designs.

The lacquer contains the same irritating substances as poison oak or poison ivy, causing some of the lacquer workers to suffer from painful rashes. Some people will even break out in a rash after handling *finished* pieces of lacquerware, even though the piece may be many years old.

Pyrethrin poison
(made from *Lonchocarpus* and *Derris*)

The Creature from the Black Lagoon is a classic science-fiction movie from the 1950s. It tells the story of a mysterious "gill-man" who is captured in a tropical lagoon by a band of explorers and taken back to the United States, where he is exhibited in an aquarium. The gill-man, of course, does not like being kept in an aquarium, so he finally smashes his tank and escapes. Were it not for his love for the beautiful heroine, the creature would certainly have destroyed half of Miami before finally disappearing into the sea.

A scene from the movie that sticks in my mind is the one in which the creature is first captured. After failing to catch the gill-man with their nets, the explorers sprinkle the surface of the lagoon with a powder they obtained from the local Indians. This powder kills the fish in the lagoon and stuns the creature so that he floats helplessly to the surface and is captured.

The Creature from the Black Lagoon is fiction, but the fish-killing powder, called *rotenone*, is real. This poisonous powder is made from the roots of a small tree that grows in parts of the West Indies and in South America. The tree is called *Lonchocarpus* by scientists and is given many different names (Timbo, Omaua, Ko-ona, for example) by native Indians. Rotenone powder will kill fish within a few minutes after being spread on the surface of the water. Fish that have been killed with rotenone powder are perfectly safe to eat. Indians have

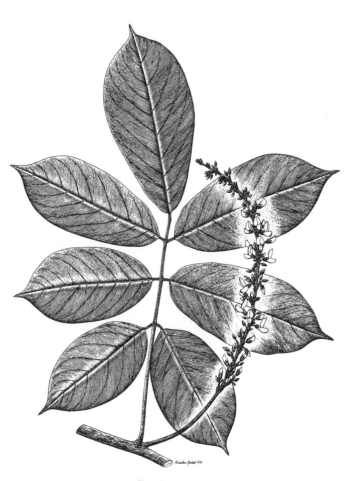

Derris
Lonchocarpus urucu

used the roots of *Lonchocarpus* in their fishing since long before European settlers came to the New World.

In East Asia and on some of the Pacific islands there grows a close relative of *Lonchocarpus*, a tree called *Derris* (both are members of the pea family). In Asia, too, the natives have used *Derris* root for fishing for thousands of years.

Until very recently, many of the insect sprays and powders had rotenone — made from both *Lonchocarpus* and *Derris* — as their major active ingredient. Today, rotenone has been replaced by synthetic organic insecticides, which are more effective in killing insects. Many of these synthetics, however, can also remain in the soil and water for many years and can harm fish, birds, and other wildlife.

Ranchers in Brazil have recently been using rotenone powder to protect their cattle against attacks by the ferocious piranha fish. The piranha is a small freshwater fish with razor-sharp teeth — it is sometimes called "the shark of the rivers." Piranhas swim in large schools. When a school of piranhas attack an animal (or a human being), they can remove all of its flesh in a matter of minutes. Cattle have sometimes had their tongues chewed off when they drank from a piranha-infested stream, and cows wading through flooded fields have had their udders severely bitten by the fish. As cattle ranchers continue to move deeper into the wildlands of Brazil, their cattle will be more and more exposed to attacks by piranha fish and so, undoubtedly, the use of rotenone will increase.

Rotenone poison

(various species of *Chrysanthemum*)

Several years ago I lived in a house that was plagued by mosquitoes. It seemed that no matter how well I kept the doors and windows screened one of these annoying insects would get into the house and bite me. When I told my neighbor about the problem, she suggested that I get something called a *mosquito coil*, a spiral-shaped device that is burned. Smoke from the mosquito coil kills mosquitoes. I tried one and it worked like a charm.

Later I learned that mosquito coils contain the natural insecticide pyrethrin, which comes from the flowers of several different species of *Chrysanthemum*. For many years pyrethrins were widely used in insect sprays, but during the 1950s and 1960s pyrethrin sprays were gradually replaced by synthetic insecticides such as DDT, malathion, and chlordane.

Today some of these synthetic insecticides are being replaced by pyrethrin because it causes less damage to the environment. Scientists have shown that DDT and other synthetic insecticides may remain in the soil for many years after they have been sprayed. Some of these synthetic insecticides have found their way into the bodies of wild birds and animals and into plants. If cows eat plants containing DDT, they can pass the poison along to people in their milk. Pyrethrins are safer because they decompose rapidly when they fall to the ground, quickly losing their poisonous properties.

Chrysanthemum
Chrysanthemum leucanthemum

Opium Poppy
(Papaver somniferum)

Toward the end of the movie *The Wizard of Oz*, Dorothy, the Cowardly Lion, the Tin Woodsman, the Scarecrow, and Toto finally see the Emerald City shimmering in the distance across a field of brilliant orange poppies. In their haste to reach the city, the travelers stray from the Yellow Brick Road and take what they think will be a short cut through the poppy field, but before they have gone far Dorothy, Toto, and the Lion fall to the ground, fast asleep. Try as they may, the Tin Woodsman and the Scarecrow are unable to awaken their friends. Luckily, while gazing into her crystal ball, the Good Witch of the North sees Dorothy's predicament. Through her magic, the Good Witch makes a snowstorm appear over the poppy field, and when the snow has covered the poppies, the three finally awake.

The movie never really tells us what kinds of poppies grow in the fields of Oz, but, no doubt, they are meant to be opium poppies. The opium poppy and sleep go together like fleas and a dog; the plant's scientific name, *Papaver somniferum*, means "poppy that brings sleep."

Long ago it was discovered that the juice of the opium poppy made a drug with the remarkable power to put people peacefully to sleep even though they were suffering from wounds, broken bones, and other painful conditions. The juice of the opium poppy is the source of some of the most powerful painkilling drugs ever known, the *opiates*, or opium drugs. For more than six thousand years these drugs have helped to relieve human

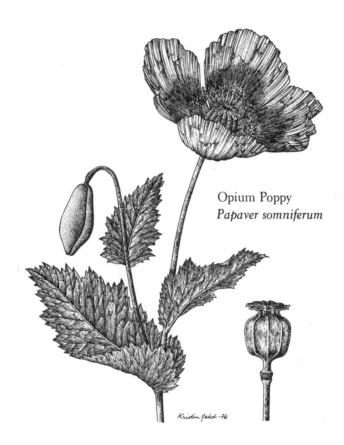

Opium Poppy
Papaver somniferum

Kristin Jakob -76

suffering. Unfortunately, these same drugs have also caused much suffering. The opium poppy is a fine example of how a poisonous plant can be both very good and very bad.

Today, most of the opiates used by doctors are synthetics — they are made from chemicals rather than extracted from the plant itself — but until 1952 all opiates were obtained directly from living poppies. One thousand tons of opium are still used in the production of medicines every year, and many more times this amount are used to make the illegal opiates, chief among which is heroin.

The strongest natural opiates are taken from the poppy a few days after its petals drop off. At the tip of each flower stalk is a swollen green seed capsule. In the walls of the capsule is a network of tiny veins that contain the narcotic juice. During an opium harvest, workers move along the rows of poppies, carefully slashing the capsule with a sharp knife. As soon as the capsule is cut, the milky white juice oozes out and is collected in buckets. The sap is then dried, usually by letting it sit in the sunlight. The dried juice is reddish brown or black in color and is called opium. One acre of opium poppies produces enough juice to make between thirty and sixty pounds of opium.

Opium in this crude form was used as a painkiller until well into the nineteenth century. Opium could be smoked in a pipe, swallowed in pills, or mixed with various liquids and drunk as a potion. Perhaps the most popular opium medicine was a potion called *laudanum*, a mixture of opium and alcohol. Laudanum was made popular by the famous German physician Paracelsus during the sixteenth century. Paracelsus's original recipe for laudanum also included powdered pearls and bits of gold. These precious ingredients did not make the medicine any stronger, but they surely made it more expensive.

Early in the nineteenth century, German chemists showed that opium was actually a mixture of several different painkilling substances, including the drugs *morphine* and *codeine*. Doctors soon discovered that pure morphine was a much more powerful painkiller than crude opium. Later in the nineteenth century, scientists at Germany's Bayer Chemical Company (the same company that makes so much aspirin today) were able to modify morphine chemically to produce the most powerful opiate of all, the drug *heroin*.

Despite all the good they have done, opiates are still very dangerous drugs. Besides their ability to deaden pain and bring sleep, all of the opiates act on the *medulla*, the part of the brain that controls a person's breathing. A strong dose of an opiate will slow the rate of breathing, and a very strong dose — an overdose — will stop breathing altogether, with death as the inevitable result.

Another problem with the opiates is their ability to create serious drug addiction. If opiates are taken over a long period of time, their dosage must be constantly increased to continue to produce the same effect. For example, if a man takes two codeine pills every six hours to deaden the pain of an earache, he may find that after a few days the pills no longer relieve his pain. Instead, he needs four pills every four hours. If something is not done to cure the man's earache (and stop the pain), he will soon need an even larger dose of codeine. Some people have managed to work themselves up to amazingly large doses of opiates in this step-by-step fashion. A morphine addict may be able to tolerate a dose of morphine two hundred times stronger than the dose needed to kill someone who is not an addict! Doctors call this phenomenon of ever-increasing dosage *tolerance*.

As a person's tolerance for opiates increases, the chemistry of the body also changes. In fact, it changes so much that when the person stops using opiates he or she may become quite sick (over and above the pain that originally made him or her start using opiates). This sickness is called *withdrawal*. Withdrawal symptoms make it very hard for a person to stop using opiates even if he or she wants to. There is only one way to prevent the unpleasant symptoms of withdrawal once they have begun: to take more opiates. The other alternative is to get sick: to experience all of the unpleasant symptoms, which may last for several days. In the long run it is better to go through withdrawal than to continue taking massive doses of opiates. But since withdrawal is such an unpleasant experience, some people prefer to continue taking drugs. At this point, they can truly be called drug addicts.

To be sure, this is not a complete explanation of why some people become drug addicts. How a person feels about himself or herself has a great deal to do with whether or not he or she becomes an addict. People with a low opinion of themselves — people who are not happy with their lives — are more likely to continue taking drugs once they start because the drugs help them to forget their unhappiness. This too is an oversimplified explanation; to explain all the reasons for people becoming drug addicts would fill several books, but in the case of the opiates their physical properties certainly have a great deal to do with addiction.

Drug addiction, especially addiction to opiates, has always been a terrible problem. During the nineteenth and early twentieth centuries hundreds of different patent medicines that contained opium or morphine were sold by American druggists. These medicines could be purchased by anyone who wanted them, since at that time there were no laws that required a doctor's signature on a prescription. Most of these opiated tonics were used to relieve aches and pains, but several (paregoric, for example) were also used to control diarrhea. (Opiates are very good for preventing diarrhea — so good, in fact, that they often cause constipation!) By far the greatest use of these patent medicines was by women who took them to relieve menstrual pain. As a result, many women became addicted to opium, codeine, or morphine. Around the turn of the century, female addicts outnumbered male addicts three to one — almost exactly the reverse of the situation that exists today.

During the Civil War (1861–1865), large amounts of morphine were used by both the Union and Confederate armies to ease the pain of battle wounds. Much of this morphine was given to the soldiers using a brand-new invention of the time: the hypodermic needle. In those days, doctors believed that drugs had to reach the stomach before they could cause addiction. They reasoned that if drugs were injected directly into the bloodstream with a hypodermic syringe there would be no problems of addiction. They were wrong. If anything, taking an opiate in this way creates an even greater tolerance for the drug. More than 400,000 men became morphine addicts during the Civil War.

Today in the United States hundreds of thousands of people are addicted to heroin. Most of these addicts began using heroin because their friends offered them the drug. Some of them began while serving in the armed forces in Vietnam, Laos, and Cambodia. In Southeast Asia heroin was plentiful and cheap and offered a way to escape the horrors of war temporarily. When these men returned to the United States they found that heroin was very expensive, and those who were addicted had no choice but to pay the price.

Because heroin is illegal, drug dealers can charge very high prices for it. Many addicts pay $50 or more every single day to support their habit. In a year they may spend more than $15,000 for heroin alone. Since heroin addicts are usually in no condition to hold a job (much less a job that pays $15,000 a year), they must get their money by "other means," which generally means burglary, robbery, or prostitution. A very large amount of the crime in the United States today, especially burglary, is committed by addicts who are desperately trying to get enough money to pay for their drugs. Much of what is glibly referred to as "the crime problem" has its roots in the poisonous plant called the opium poppy.

Besides contributing to crime, heroin addiction also causes terrible problems for the addict himself. Because much of their time is spent in getting a steady supply of heroin, addicts often neglect to eat properly or to take care of their own health. The hypodermic needles that are used to inject heroin into the bloodstream can also transmit diseases from one addict to another. There are very few heroin addicts over forty years of age for the simple reason that by then the majority of addicts have died, gone to prison, or, one hopes, somehow have been able to give up their habit.

Mandrake

(Mandragora officinarum)

The poisonous mandrake is a member of the Nightshade family. Like belladonna and other poisonous nightshades, mandrake contains the alkaloids atropine and scopolamine, and produces symptoms similar to those of belladonna poisoning. Mandrake is a small plant, standing about a foot high, with greenish yellow flowers and a long, thick root. A native of Europe, the plant has never been successfully introduced into the United States except for its presence in a few botanical gardens.

NOTE: The native American plant *Podophyllum peltatum* (the May apple) is sometimes given the common name "mandrake" though it is not at all related to the European mandrake. May apple is also a poisonous plant, however. It is an herb, about a foot high with a white flower some two inches in diameter. The plant is found throughout the United States and in southern Canada. The root is the most poisonous part of the May apple, causing violent purging (diarrhea) when eaten. The berries are less poisonous, but still dangerous, especially to children. Indians and early settlers of North America used May apple as a laxative.

The mandrake has been a favorite herb of sorcerers and witches for thousands of years and there are many legends about the

Mandrake
Mandragora officinarium

plant's magic properties. Some of these legends concern the plant's root, which many people believed was shaped like the human body.

Many legends tell of the mandrake's power in love potions. In the Old Testament, in Genesis 30:14–16, is the story of Rachel and how she used the mandrake as a love charm. During the Middle Ages there was such a great demand for mandrake root that some dishonest plant merchants substituted the roots of other plants that they had carved into the shape of human figures.

Extracts of the mandrake were thought to cure almost every imaginable disease. In a very entertaining book, *Nightshades: The Paradoxical Plants*, botanist Charles Heiser reports that one medieval author wrote that mandrake "cures every infirmity — except only death . . ."

Other legends told how the mandrake would give out a blood-curdling scream when it was pulled from the ground. Some people believed that mandrakes glowed in the dark, and thus the best time to hunt for the plant was at night. Mandrakes were also believed to grow underneath a hangman's gallows; if a man had been hanged, the mandrake was supposed to take the form of a man, and if a woman was hanged, the plant would take her form. Today, the legend of the magic mandrake lives on in the comic strips in the character of one "Mandrake the Magician."

Lathyrus sativus

(*Lathyrus sativus*)

In June 1975 a severe drought struck India, causing crop failures throughout the states of Madhya Pradesh and Bihar. Millions of people faced starvation. As they had done many times before, the farmers of Madhya Pradesh and Bihar responded by planting crops of a pea plant called *kesari dal*, which thrives even on dry, unirrigated soil. As had also happened many times before, the results of planting this crop were disastrous — *kesari dal* is a poisonous plant that leaves its victims permanently crippled and sometimes dead. This poisoning is called *lathyrism*, from the Latin name of the plant, *Lathyrus sativus*. During the 1975 drought in India, there were more than 100,000 victims of lathyrism in these two states alone. (You may wonder why the farmers grew a plant that was known to be poisonous. For those of us who live comfortably and always have enough to eat, the answer may be difficult to understand. To the farmers it made perfect sense: given the choice between starvation, which was certain, and poisoning, which was less certain, they chose not to starve.)

Lathyrus sativus is unusual among poisonous plants in that almost all of its victims are men between the ages of fifteen and forty-five. Women, children, and older men are spared, though no one knows for sure why this happens. Some scientists believe that the poisons in *kesari dal* must somehow react with male sex hormones to become effective. But cattle, sheep,

Locoweed
Lathyrus sativus

and horses of both sexes may also be poisoned from eating too much of this plant, so hormones may not be the answer.

The first symptom of lathyrism is trouble in walking. The victim's steps become short and jerky. In time his knees become bent, his heels raise, and he is forced to walk on his toes. In its advanced stages, lathyrism leaves victims permanently paralyzed below the hips. In very severe cases the arms are also paralyzed, and in its most severe form lathyrism ends in death.

Before symptoms become visible, the victims must consume large amounts of the poisonous pea. If a person subsists on a diet that is nearly all *kesari dal*, the first symptoms will be seen in between four and eight weeks. With smaller proportions of the seed in the diet the symptoms will take longer to appear. If the pea supplies less than one third of the diet, symptoms are usually never seen. Unfortunately, in times of drought and famine people may subsist on diets that are extremely high in *Lathyrus sativus*. During the 1975 Indian drought many poor laborers were given a daily ration of *Lathyrus* seeds rather than cash wages.

Today, most epidemics of lathyrism are confined to India and neighboring countries, but in the past they have been seen in Britain, France, Italy, Spain, North Africa, and Russia. Two factors that always contribute to a lathyrism epidemic are drought and poverty.

Recently chemists have discovered the poisonous substance in *Lathyrus sativus*, a chemical with the impressive name "beta-N-oxalyl-alpha-beta-diamino propionic acid." Most of this poisonous compound can be cooked out of the seeds with hot water. Today in India health workers are going into the countryside, demonstrating to farmers how they can make *kesari dal* safe to eat.

BIBLIOGRAPHY

Arena, J. M. *Poisoning*, 3rd ed., Springfield, Ill.: Charles C Thomas, 1974.

Blyth, A. W., and Blyth, M. W. *Poisons: Their Effects and Detection.* London: Charles Griffin and Co., 1924.

Bryn, T. K. *Curare: Its History and Usage.* Philadelphia: J. B. Lippincott, 1963.

Cutting, W. C. *Handbook of Pharmacology*, 3rd ed. New York: Appleton-Century-Crofts, 1969.

Emboden, W. A., Jr. *Narcotic Plants.* New York: Macmillan, 1972.

Hardin, J. W., and Arena, J. M. *Human Poisoning from Native and Cultivated Plants.* Durham: Duke University Press, 1969.

Heiser, C. B. *Nightshades: The Paradoxical Plants.* San Francisco: W. H. Freeman, 1969.

Hutner, S. H., and McLaughlin, J. "Poisonous Tides." *Scientific American* 199 (August 1958).

Jensen, L. B. *Poisoning Misadventures.* Springfield, Ill.: Charles C Thomas, 1970.

Keeton, W. T. *Biological Science*, 3rd ed. New York: W. W. Norton, 1972.

Kingsbury, J. M. *Deadly Harvest: A Guide to Common Poisonous Plants.* New York: Holt, Rinehart, and Winston, 1965.

———. *Poisonous Plants of the United States and Canada.* Englewood, N.J.: Prentice-Hall, 1964.

Krieger, L. C. C. *The Mushroom Handbook.* New York: Dover, 1967.

Lees, C. B. *Gardens, Plants, and Man.* Englewood, N.J.: Prentice-Hall, 1970.

Litten, W. "The Most Poisonous Mushrooms." *Scientific American* 232 (March 1975).

Muenscher, W. C. *Poisonous Plants of the United States.* New York: Macmillan, 1940.

Natarajan, K. R. India's Poison Peas. *Chemistry* 49, no. 6, 1976.

National Clearinghouse for Poison Control Centers. *Bulletin* October 1976. Washington, D.C.: U.S. Department of Health, Education and Welfare, 1976.

———. *Poison Control Statistics 1974.* Washington, D.C.: U.S. Department of Health, Education and Welfare, 1976.

Raloff, J. Poison Peas Around the World. *Chemistry* 49, no. 6, 1976.

"The Red Tide — A Public Health Emergency." *The New England Journal of Medicine* 288 (May 24, 1973): 1126.

Roberts, D. A., and Boothroyd, C. W. *Fundamentals of Plant Pathology*. San Francisco: W. H. Freeman, 1972.

Schleiffer, H., ed. *Sacred Narcotic Plants of the New World Indians*. New York: Hafner, 1973.

Shumaker, W. *The Occult Sciences in the Renaissance: A Study in Intellectual Patterns*. Berkeley: University of California Press, 1972.

Stephenson, J., and Churchill, J. M. *Medical Botany*, vol. 1–3. London: John Churchill, 1834–36.

Steyn, D. G. *The Toxicology of Plants in South Africa*. Durban: South Africa Central News Agency, 1934.

Watt, J. M., and Breyer-Brandwijk, M. G. *The Medicinal and Poisonous Plants of Southern and Eastern Africa*, 2nd ed. Edinburgh: E. and S. Livingstone, 1962.

Weiner, M. A. *Earth Medicines, Earth Foods*. New York: Macmillan, 1972.

Wilson, C. L., and Loomis, W. E. *Botany*, 4th ed. New York: Holt, Rinehart, and Winston, 1967.